Secundum fidem vestram

fiat vobis.

©2021 Catherine Fet · North Landing Books · All rights reserved

Ecclesiastical Latin – Pronunciation

The pronunciation of **Ecclesiastical Latin** is a little different from **Classical Latin**. It is actually quite similar to modern Italian.

Most **consonants** are pronounced just as they are in English:

c = [k] as in 'cat'
g = [g] as in 'go'
qu = as [kw]

Exceptions:
c before *e* and *i* is pronounced as [ch] – ***principio*** = [principio]
g before *e* and *i* is pronounced as [j] – ***argentum*** = [arjentum]
j is pronounced as [y] – Judas = [yudas]
t before *ia, io, iu* is pronounced as [ts]

Vowels:
a = as in 'father'
o = as in 'not'
e = as in 'pet'
u = as in 'put'
i = as in 'pit'

Vowels that occur together are pronounced as two separate vowels:
Deus – [de-oos].
There are a few special vowel combinations – diphthongs:
ae is pronounced as [ai] – as in 'bye'
au is pronounced as in 'house'
eu is pronounced as 'yew'
oe – as in 'foil'

rēgīna – *ī* is long; it is stressed (˙)
domina – *i* is short, the stress is on the 3rd syllable from the end

Stress: In Latin, the stress falls on either the second or the third syllable from the end of the word. In the days of Ancient Rome some vowels in Latin were short and some were long. If the second syllable from the end had a long vowel, that syllable was stressed. I will mark the long/short vowels, or the stressed syllable in frequently used longer words.

Beati qui non viderunt, et crediderunt.

Nisi videro in manibus eius figuram clavorum, et mittam digitum meum in locum clavorum, et mittam manum meam in latus eius, non credam!

'Doubting Thomas' by Caravaggio

Below are the *Ten Commandments* (Deut.5) and a passage from the *Sermon on the Mount* with the grammar commentary and color coding you will find throughout this textbook. As your knowledge grows, and you learn to recognize more and more Latin grammatical forms and vocabulary, come back to this page to celebrate your progress!

Genitive ▬▬   Ablative ▬▬   Accusative ▬▬   Dative ▬▬   Vocative ▬▬

I.   Ego sum Dominus Deus tuus. Non habebis deos alienos in conspectu meo.
II.   Non usurpabis nomen Domini Dei tui frustra.
III.   Observa diem sabbati.   **cōnspectus, cōnspectūs,** m. (4) – sight
IV.   Honora patrem tuum et matrem tuam.   **fūrtum, fūrtī,** n. (2) – theft >> furtive
V.   Non occides.   **uxor, uxōris,** f. (3) – wife
VI.   Non moechaberis.
VII. *Furtumque non facies.*
VIII. Nec loqueris contra proximum tuum falsum testimonium.   AGER   DOMUS
IX.   Non concupisces uxorem proximi tui.
X.   Non concupisces domum, non agrum, non servum... proximi tui.

Simple Future:
habebis – *habeō, habēre, habuī, habitum* (2) – to have
usurpabis – *ūsūrpō, ūsūrpāre, ūsūrpāvī, ūsūrpātum* (1) – to use, to seize
occides – *occīdō, occīdere, occīdī, occīsum* (3) – to murder
moechaberis – *moechor, moechārī, moechātum* (dep.) – to be unfaithful
facies – *faciō, facere, fēcī, factum* (3) – to make, to do
loqueris – *loquor, loquī, locūtum* (dep.) – to talk, to speak
concupisces – *concupīscō, concupīscere, concupīvī, concupītum* (3.) – to desire

BONUS — MALUS
IUSTUS — INIUSTUS
AMICUS — INIMICUS
AMOR — ODIUM

CAELUS
NUBES
SOL

Imperative Mood:
observa – *observō, observāre, observāvī, observātum* (1) – to observe
honora – *honōrō, honōrāre, honōrāvī, honōrātum* (1) – to honor

Audistis quia dictum est: diliges proximum tuum, et odio habebis inimicum tuum.
Ego autem dico vobis: diligite inimicos vestros, benefacite his qui oderunt vos, et orate
pro persequentibus et calumniantibus vos. Ut sitis filii Patris vestri qui in caelis est
qui solem suum oriri facit super bonos et malos et pluit super iustos et iniustos.
Si enim diligatis eos qui vos diligunt quam mercedem habebitis? (Matt. 5)

PLUIT

Past Perfect: *audistis* (*audire*); **Past Participle:** *dictum* (*dicere*); **Simple Future:** *diliges* (*diligere* = love), *habebis, habebitis* (*habere*); **Subjunctive Present:** *sitis* (*esse*) – 'so that you are'

Lesson I

Salve! Let's begin our first class with Latin nouns.
Good news first: There are no articles, like *the* or *a/an* in Latin!

And now the bad news: Unlike English nouns, all Latin nouns have gender – **masculine, feminine,** or **neuter**. For some nouns the gender is obvious:
Pater – father – is masculine. *Mater* – mother – is feminine.
Filius – son – is masculine. *Filia* – daughter – is feminine.
Rex – king – is masculine. *Regina* – queen – is feminine.
Dominus – lord – is masculine. *Domina* – lady – is feminine.
Deus – God – is masculine. *Spīritus* – spirit is masculine.

AGNUS DEI

baptismus – baptism
baptisterium – baptistry
Iohannes Baptista – John the Baptist

However, not only living beings have gender in Latin. Things and ideas have gender too!
Ecclesia – church – is feminine. *Liber* – book – is masculine.
Sacramentum – sacrament – is neuter. *Templum* – temple – is neuter.
Fortunately, it's easy to tell the gender of a noun by its ending.
Most masculine nouns end in **- us, - er, - ir** – *dominus, pater, Deus, filius...*
Most feminine nouns end in **- a** – *regina, ecclesia, filia...*
Most neuter nouns end in **- um** – *sacramentum, templum...*

CALIX SALŪTĀRIS

You will have to do some memorization, however, because quite a few endings are shared by nouns of different genders, for example:
lux – light – feminine • *crux* – cross – feminine • *calix* – chalice – masculine
Dictionaries use abbreviations **m.** for masculine, **f.** for feminine, and **n.** for neuter.

INCENSUM

INCENSORIUM – A CENSER

By the end of the 4th century the split of the Roman Empire into the Eastern and Western empires became final. Latin was the language of the Western Roman Empire, and Greek was the language of the Eastern Roman Empire. Until then the primary language of the Church had been Greek. When St. Paul wrote to the Church in Rome, he wrote in Greek. However, following the split, Greek was used less and less in the Western Roman Empire, and soon Latin emerged as the language of the Western Church. Ecclesiastical or Church Latin absorbed the conversational Latin of the late Roman era. By the 9th century it became the international language of education, arts, and law in medieval Europe.

And here is why you need to remember the gender of nouns. Latin nouns change their forms based on their gender and number (singular or plural). While the plural forms of most English nouns end in -s, Latin nouns have different plural endings depending on their gender.

Masculine nouns ending in *- us, - er, - ir* change to *- i* or *- es* ending in their plural forms:
dominus – lord; *domini* – lords
Deus – God; *dei* – gods
filius – son; *filii* – sons
pater – father; *patres* – fathers
Feminine nouns ending in *- a* change to *- ae* ending in plural:
domina – lady; *dominae* – ladies
ecclesia – church; *ecclesiae* – churches
Neuter nouns ending in *- um* change to *- a* ending in plural:
sacramentum – sacrament; *sacramenta* – sacraments
templum – temple; *templa* – temples
donum – gift; *dona* – gifts

Sanctus Spiritus – the Holy Spirit
Dominus Sanctus – the Holy Lord
Aeternus Deus – Eternal God
Deus vivus – Living God
gloria aeterna – eternal glory
Sancta Ecclesia Catholica – the Holy Catholic Church
Sancta Familia – the Holy Family
Curia Romana – the Papal Court
sapientia aeterna – eternal wisdom

Not too difficult, but, of course, there are other, less common singular and plural endings!

Another reason to know the gender of nouns is the habit of Latin adjectives to copy the endings of nouns. In English adjectives don't change at all: good son – good sons. But Latin nouns change their endings based on the gender and number of nouns they describe.
filius bonus – good son – m. singular
filii boni – good sons – m. plural
As you see, the adjective *bonus* simply copycats the *- us* (singular) and *- i* (plural) endings of the masculine noun it describes.
With feminine nouns, adjectives copycat the endings *- a* (singular) and *- ae* (plural); and with neuter nouns, they echo the endings *- um* (singular) and *- a* (plural).

terra magna f. >> *terrae magnae* – great lands
magnus opus n. >> *magna opera* – great deeds
parvulus beatus m. >> *parvuli beati* – blessed little ones
angelus sanctus m. >> *angeli sancti* – holy angels

Collegium Sacrum – the College of Cardinals

Pax et Bonum – Peace and Good (Franciscan motto)

Vulgata

St. Jerome was an accomplished scholar. He was fluent in Greek and knew some Hebrew. To improve his understanding of the Old Testament St. Jerome moved to Israel. He translated some books of the Old and New Testaments of the Bible himself. For other books he selected good existing Latin translations, revised them, and added them to his version of the Bible. He completed his work between AD 382 and 405, in Bethlehem. In his translation of the Bible St. Jerome used the popular style of Latin, not the scholarly or poetic Latin typical of the written texts of that era. Clarity was more important to him than elegance of style. Over the years St. Jerome's translation became more popular than older Latin versions of the Bible, and was nicknamed *versio vulgata* – 'a common version' of the Latin Bible, or just *Vulgata*.

LIBER

HIERONYMUS SCRIBIT.

'St. Jerome in his study' by Domenico Ghirlandaio

Past participles behave like adjectives. For example, **benedictus, benedicta, benedictum** = blessed, is a past participle formed from the Latin verb **benedicere** – to bless (**bene** = well + **dicere** = say).
Missa Lecta – the Mass that is read << *lecta* – Past Participle formed from from *legere* – to read
Missa Cantata – the Mass that is sung << *cantata* – Past Participle formed from *cantare* – to sing

What if our nouns don't have these most common endings, *- us, - a, - um*? What if these are *pater*, *mater*, or *nomen*? Will adjectives copycat these other endings? No! Thank God (*Deo gratias!*). Most Latin adjectives stick to the more familiar model:

masculine singular *- us*, masculine plural *- i*
feminine singular *- a*, feminine plural *- ae*
neuter singular *- um*, neuter plural *- a*

capella – chapel
capellanus – chaplain
catechismus – catechism

E.g. (exempli gratia = for example):
pastor bonus – good shepherd (m. singular) • *Beata Mater* – Blessed Mother (f. singular)
nomen sanctum – the holy name (n. singular) • *panis verus* – true bread (m. singular)
Mater Sanctissima – the Most Holy Mother (f. singular) • *sancta nox* – holy night (f. singular)
sancta Trinitas – the Holy Trinity (f. singular) • *plebs sancta* – holy people (f. singular)
sanguis pretiosissimus – the most precious blood (m. singular)
Doctor Angelicus – the Angelic Doctor (St. Thomas Aquinas) (m. singular)
Lex mala, lex nulla – A bad law is no law (St. Thomas Aquinas) (f. singular)

Let's take a look at a few sentences from the *Laudes Divinae* (*The Divine Praises*) and notice the way adjectives and past participles choose the more common endings.

Benedictus Deus. – Blessed be God.

Benedictum Nomen Sanctum eius. – Blessed be His Holy Name (*eius* = his).

[Notice that **nomen** = name doesn't have the **-um** ending, but **benedictum** and **sanctum** do, because **nomen** is masculine.]

Benedictus Iesus Christus, verus Deus et verus homo.
Blessed be Jesus Christ, true God and true Man.

[**homo** = man doesn't have the **-us** ending, but the adjective **verus** does, because **homo** is masculine.]

Benedictum Nomen Iesu. – Blessed be the Name of Jesus.

Benedictum Cor eius sacratissimum.
Blessed be His Most Sacred Heart.

[**cor** = heart doesn't have the **-um** ending, but **benedictum** does, because **cor** is neuter.]

Benedictus Sanguis eius pretiosissimus.
Blessed be His Most Precious Blood.

[**sanguis** = blood is masculine]

*Benedicta excelsa Mater Dei,
Maria sanctissima.*
Blessed be the great Mother of God, Mary most Holy.

'The Annunciation' by Sassetta, 1435
Church mosaic from Ravenna, AD 425

But, as you have already figured out, Latin is a tricky language.
So adjectives are not as simple as we would like them to be.
Some masculine adjectives end in - *er*;
some masculine and feminine adjectives end in - *is*;
some neuter adjectives end in - *e*;
And there are other variations.

sacer, sacra, sacrum – sacred >> *musica sacra* – sacred music
dexter, dextra, dextrum – right >> *dextra manus* – the right hand
cor triste – sorrowful heart (neuter) • *Missa Solemnis* – the Solemn Mass

**BIBLIA =
VETUS TESTAMENTUM +
NOVUM TESTAMENTUM**

READING from the *Creed of St. Athanasius*

Qualis Pater, talis Filius, talis Spiritus Sanctus.
Such as the Father is; such is the Son; and such is the Holy Ghost.
Increatus Pater, increatus Filius, increatus Spiritus Sanctus.
The Father uncreated; the Son uncreated; and the Holy Ghost uncreated.
Immensus Pater, immensus Filius, immensus Spiritus Sanctus.
The Father unlimited; the Son unlimited; and the Holy Ghost unlimited.
Aeternus Pater, aeternus Filius, aeternus Spiritus Sanctus.
The Father eternal; the Son eternal; and the Holy Ghost eternal.
Et tamen non tres aeterni, sed unus aeternus.
And yet they are not three eternals; but one eternal.
*Sicut non tres increati, nec tres immensi, sed unus increatus,
et unus immensus.* As also there are not three uncreated; nor three
infinites, but one uncreated; and one infinite.
Similiter, omnipotens Pater, omnipotens Filius, omnipotens Spiritus Sanctus.
So likewise the Father is Almighty; the Son Almighty; and the Holy Ghost Almighty.
Et tamen non tres omnipotentes, sed unus omnipotens.
And yet they are not three Almighties; but one Almighty.
Ita Deus Pater, Deus Filius, Deus Spiritus Sanctus. Et tamen non tres Dii, sed unus est Deus.
So the Father is God; the Son is God; and the Holy Ghost is God.
And yet they are not three Gods; but one God.
Ita Dominus Pater, Dominus Filius, Dominus Spiritus Sanctus.
So likewise the Father is Lord; the Son Lord; and the Holy Ghost Lord.
Et tamen non tres Domini, sec Unus est Dominus.
And yet not three Lords; but one Lord.

PERIMUS!

MARE

DISCIPULI

DOMINUS

UBI EST FIDES VESTRA?

Sola Scriptura –
Scripture Alone:
the fundamental point
of dispute in the
Protestant Reformation
solus – only, alone
scriptura – book

LESSON II

> Latin – **Deus** >> deity
> Greek – θεός – [Theos]
> >> theology, theological

We begin this class with Latin personal pronouns:

I	*ego*	we	*nos*
you	*tu*	you (plural)	*vos*
he	*is*	they (m.)	*ei*
she	*ea*	they (f.)	*eae*
it	*id*	they (n.)	*ea*

Everything here looks familiar except for the three 'they' pronouns – different for each gender, but using the familiar plural noun endings - *i* (m.) - *ae* (f.), - *a* (n.)

Latin possessive pronouns are actually adjectives. They use standard adjective endings:
meus, mea, meum – my >> *Deus meus* – My God; *oratio mea* (f.) – my prayer
tuus, tua, tuum – your (singular) >> *filius tuus* – your son; *servi tui* – your servants (*servus*, m.)
noster, nostra, nostrum – our >> *mater nostra* – our mother
vester, vestra, vestrum – your (plural) >> *donum vestrum* (n.) – your gift

REX ET REGINA

A few examples from the *Lord's Prayer*:
Pater Noster – Our Father • **nomen tuum** – your name (n., singular)
regnum tuum – your kingdom (n., singular) • **voluntas tua** – your will (f., singular)
debita nostra – our debts (*debitum* - n., singular; *debita* - plural)

Beati pauperes quia vestrum est regnum Dei. (Luke 6:20)
Blessed are the poor, for yours is the kingdom of God.

> *Deus Revelatus* – the Revealed God
> *Deus Absconditus* – the Hidden God

So far so good, but... leave it to Latin to make things more complicated than necessary! The ancient Romans must have had a lot of time on their hands to come up with all those grammatical forms! Latin has two different ways of saying **his, her, its, their**. When something/someone belongs to the subject of the sentence, use
suus/sua/suum – his/her/its own
The king gave Jesus his (king's) gift.
donum suum – 'his own gift' – the gift that belonged to the king, the subject of this sentence
When something/someone does not belong to the subject of the sentence, use
eius (his, her, its)
His gift was gold.
donum eius – his gift; the subject of the sentence is 'gold,' not 'king'

> *Cantus Gregorianus* – Gregorian chant
> *cantus*, m. – song

Here are some examples, again, from the *Laudes Divinae:*

Benedictus Sanguis eius pretiosissimus.

Blessed be His Most Precious Blood.

(In this sentence Jesus is not the subject of the sentence; the subject is *Sanguis*.)

Benedictus Deus. Benedictum Nomen Sanctum eius.

Blessed be God. Blessed be His Holy Name.

(In the second sentence *Deus* is not the subject of the sentence; the subject is *Nomen*.)

Benedictus Deus in Angelis suis, et in Sanctis suis. Amen.

Blessed be God in His Angels and in His Saints.

(*Deus* = subject)

Continuing the theme of 'what's hard in Latin,' let's face one of the most difficult areas – the Latin **declension**. Declension is nouns changing form depending on their gender, number, or role in a sentence. In English nouns don't 'decline,' only pronouns change their forms:

I, he, she, we, they, who = subject forms, where a pronoun is the subject of the sentence

me, him, her, them, whom = object forms, where a pronoun is a direct or indirect object

In Latin, as nouns and pronouns change their forms, these changes are organized into **cases**. There are six cases. Each includes singular and plural forms for each gender – masculine, feminine, and neuter.

For English speakers it's certainly a lot to process. But don't panic! Many of these forms are the same, and you'll grasp them all in no time! So, fortitude!

The six Latin cases are: **Nominative, Genitive, Dative, Accusative, Ablative, and Vocative.** All Latin nouns can be grouped into five types, or **declensions**. Dictionaries always indicate the declension group for each noun.

For example *pater* (3) – 3rd declension

Nominative case is the main form of a noun – its 'subject' form. All other cases are called 'oblique.'

Ego sum Alpha et Omega.

Ego sum Dominus Deus tuus.

Genitive Case

Simply put, whenever you use the preposition 'of,' or possessive forms (friend's, father's, mother's) in English, Latin uses Genitive case, without a preposition.
Agnus Dei – Lamb of God • *verbum Dei* – word of God • *imago Dei* – image of God
stella natalis – the star of Nativity • *Corpus Christi* – Body of Christ • *vox Dei* – voice of God

Here is a chart of the singular and plural endings in the Nominative and Genitive cases. Notice that nouns of different declensions have different endings in Genitive case.

Declension	Nominative Case ending	Genitive Singular	Genitive Plural
1st	-a	- ae	- arum
2nd	-us, -r, -er, -ir, - um	- i	- orum
3rd	-x, -s , - is, - e, - n & more	- is	- um, - ium
4th	-us	- us	- uum
5th	-es	- ei	- erum

Important! Latin nouns sometimes change their stem as they change from case to case. They can have one stem in the Nominative case, and a different stem in all other cases. Dictionaries usually list two forms for Latin nouns – Nominative and Genitive. The Genitive case form shows any stem change. Dictionaries also indicate gender and declension:
veritas, veritatis, f. (3) – truth • Here *veritas* is the Nominative case form, and *veritatis* is the Genitive case form showing that the stem for most of this word's forms is *veritat*. From this point on, I will list each new word in dictionary format, as shown above.

SINGULAR: Genitive case nouns are underlined in red
Signum Crucis – the Sign of the Cross – *crux, crucis*, f. (3)
sanguis Domini – Blood of [our] Lord – *dominus, dominī*, m. (2); *pax Domini* – peace of the Lord
dies natalis – birthday – *nātālis, nātālis*, m. (3) – birth • *acta sanctorum* – the acts of the saints
advocatus diaboli – devil's advocate – *diabolus, diabolī*, m. (2)
lux lucis – light of light – *lūx, lūcis*, f. (3) • *acta martyrum* – the acts of the martyrs
fons luminis – the source (fountain) of light – *lūmen, lūminis*, n. (3)
historia salutis – the history of salvation – *salūs, salūtis*, f. (3) - salvation
Rex gloriae – the king of glory – *glōria, glōriae*, f. (1) • *Locus Calvariae* – the place of the skull
peccata mundi – the sins of the world – *mundus, mundī*, m. (2)
mysteria fidei – mysteries of the faith – *fidēs, fideī*, f. (5)

PLURAL: Genitive case:

Iēsus Nazarēnus, Rēx Iūdæōrum (INRI) – Jesus the Nazarene, King of the Jews –
  iūdaeus, iūdaeī, m. (2) – a Jew
communio sanctorum – Communion of the Saints – *sānctus, sānctī*, m. (2) – a saint
servus servorum Dei – servant of the servants of God (Pope / bishop) –
  servus, servī, m. (2) – servant, slave
redemptio animarum – the salvation of souls – *anima, animae*, f. (1)
Rex angelorum – King of angels – *angelus, angelī*, m. (2)
Rex caelorum – King of the heavens – *caelus, caelī*, m. (2)
secula seculorum – ages of ages

Sensus Dīvīnitās – The sense of divinity: All people know that God exists. *dīvīnitās, dīvīniātis*, f. (3) – divinity

You will find a lot of Genitive case nouns in the *Litany of the Most Holy Name of Jesus*:
splendor Patris – splendor of the Father – *pater, patris*, m. (3)
Rex gloriae – King of glory
sol justitiae – Sun of righteousness – *iūstitia, iūstitiae*, f. (1)
Deus pacis – God of peace – *pāx, pācis*, f. (3)
auctor vitae – author of life
magister apostolorum – Master (Teacher) of the apostles – *apostolus, apostolī*, m. (2)

A.D. = anno Domini
A.A.C. = anno ante Christum Natum = B.C.

Pronouns also have case forms. Remember *eius* from the *Laudes Divinae*?
It's the Genitive case of *is/ea/id* = he/she/it >> of her/of him/of it.

Annulus Piscatoris
ānnulus, ānnulī, m. (2) - ring
piscatoris = Genitive case of *piscātor, piscātōris*, m. (3) – fisherman

The Ring of the Fisherman, also known as the Piscatory Ring, is a ring worn by the Pope. Each Pope has his own signet ring with his name in Latin. Traditionally, the signet image on the ring features St. Peter fishing from a boat. The ring was used to seal documents signed by the Pope until 1842.

Pont.Max = Pontifex Maximus – Pope, or the chief high priest (a position in ancient Rome)
pontifex, pontificis, m. (3) – high priest, bishop

Declension of Adjectives and Possessive Pronouns

Adjectives are copycats! They echo noun endings in the Genitive and other cases, just like they copy them in the Nominative case. Most adjectives belong to the 1st and 2nd declensions, end in - *a*, - *us*, - *r*, - *um*, and copy the endings of the 1st and 2nd declension nouns.
panis sanctus vitae aeternae – the holy bread of life everlasting – *vīta, vītae,* f. (1)
calix salutis perpetuae – the chalice of eternal salvation
Iustorum autem animae in manu Dei sunt. (Wisdom 3:1)
But the souls of the righteous are in the hand of God.
iustorum << masculine, plural Genitive case of *iustus*

CORONA DE SPINIS

However, 3rd declension adjectives are quite common too. The most common 3rd declension adjective endings are:
- *er* (m.) – *celeber* – famous
- *is* (m., f.) – *mirabilis* – amazing, miraculous, *caelestis* – heavenly, *fidelis* – faithful
- *e* (n.) – *breve* – short, *simile* – similar
- *ox*, - *ax*, -*ix* – *ferox* – ferocious, *felix* – happy
These nouns copy the 3rd declension noun endings in the Genitive case.

PECCATUM ORIGINALE

Possessive pronouns behave like adjectives of the 1st and 2nd declensions.
Memoriam fecit mirabilium suorum, misericors et miserator Dominus. (Ps.110:4)
He has made a remembrance of his wonderful works, being a merciful and gracious Lord.
...*memoriam venerantes omnium sanctorum tuorum*...
...venerating the memory of all Your saints...

Ablative Case

Our next case is Ablative. It is used with many prepositions common in Church Latin, like
in = in • *cum* = with • *ex* = from • *pro* = for • *de* = from, of • *a/ab* = from, away, by
In other words, prepositions *in, cum, ex, pro, de* and some others will make any noun following them change its form to Ablative case.
ex cathedra – 'from the chair' (of St. Peter)
In nomine Patris et Filii et Spiritus Sancti.
In the Name of the Father and of the Son and of the Holy Ghost.
(*nomine* – Ablative case of *nōmen, nōminis,* n. (3); *Patris, Filii, Spiritus Sancti* – Genitive case)

Summum Bonum – the Ultimate Good = the glory of God

Declension	Nominative	Ablative Singular	Ablative Plural
1st	-a	-a	-is
2nd	-us, -r, -er, -ir, -um	-o	-is
3rd	-x, -s, -is, -e, -n & more	-e, -i	-ibus
4th	-us	-u	-ibus
5th	-es	-e	-ebus

Genitive –   Ablative –

De corde enim exeunt cogitationes malae. (Matt. 15:19) – For out of the heart come evil thoughts.
Justus ex fide vivet. (Gal. 3:11) – The righteous will live by faith.
Igitur ex fructibus eorum cognoscetis eos. (Matt. 7:20) – Therefore by their fruits you shall know them.
Quis nos separabit a caritate Christi? (Rom. 8:35) – Who shall separate us from the love of Christ?
a caritate – Ablative case – *cāritās, cāritātis*, f. (3) – charity, love
de profundis – from the depths – *profundis* = plural Ablative of *profundus* (adjective) – deep
pro nobis – for us – *nobis* = Ablative of *nos* – we
natus ex Maria Virgine – born of/from the Virgin Mary – *virgō, virginis*, f. (3)
Libera nos ab omni malo, omni peccato... – Deliver us from all evil, all sin...
malum, malī, n (2) – evil; *peccātum, peccātī*, n (2) – sin; *omnis* – all
mea culpa, mea maxima culpa – through/by my fault – *culpa, culpae*, f (1)
in diebus Herodis regis Iudaeae – in the days of Herod, the king of Judaea – *diēs, diēī*, f, m. (5)
Et respondit ad illum Iesus: scriptum est quia non in pane solo vivet homo sed in omni verbo Dei.
(Luke 4:4) – And Jesus answered him, saying, it is written that man shall not live by bread alone, but by every word of God. – *in pane* – *pānis, pānis*, m. (3), *in verbo* – *verbum, verbī*, n. (2)
Et panis, quem ego dabo, caro mea est pro mundi vita. (John 6:51)
This bread is my flesh, which I will give for the life of the world.
During the mass, when the priest says the words of the sacramental rite, he acts
in persona Christi – 'in the person of Christ,' or as/on behalf of Christ.
in persona – Ablative case of *persona* f. – character, role; *persona Christi* – Genitive case of *Christus*
Pater Noster, qui es in caelis, sanctificetur nomen tuum.
Adveniat regnum tuum. Fiat voluntas tua, sicut in caelo et in terra.
in caelis – Ablative plural case of *caelus, caelī*, m. (2) – sky
in terra – Ablative singular case of *terra, terrae* f. (1) – land

a.m.c. – *a mundo condito*
from the creation of the world

Foedus – Covenant
foedus novum –
New Covenant, Testament
foedus, foederis, n. (3) – treaty
>> federal, federation

A special use of the Ablative case is 'by name':
Mattheum nomine. (Matt.9:9) – Matthew by name.

Preposition *cum* can appear either as a word in its own right, or attached to one of the words it connects. Here is a dialog you hear at mass:
Dominus Vobiscum.
May the Lord be with you.
(literally: the Lord with you)
vobiscum = *cum vobis*
(the Ablative case of *vos* – you)
Et cum spiritu tuo.
And with your Spirit.
(*spiritu* – Ablative case of *spiritus*, m., *tuo* – Ablative case of *tuus*)
Pax Domini sit semper vobiscum.
May the peace of the Lord be always with you.

Ave Maria, gratia plena, Dominus tecum.
Hail Mary, full of Grace, the Lord is with you.
Divinum auxilium maneat semper nobiscum.
May the divine assistance remain always with us.

'The Adoration of the Shepherds' by Bartolo di Fredi, 1374

There is another word in Latin that attaches itself to one of the words it links – the conjunction – *que* = and. For example, in **Symbolum Nicaenum** (*The Nicene Creed*), we find the words:
Credo... in Spiritum Sanctum... qui ex Patre Filioque procedit.
I believe... in the Holy Spirit... Who proceeds from the Father and the Son.
Filioque is the Ablative case of *filius* – son, with the *que* attached to it.

Et relictis retibus, secuti sunt eum.

READING

The Sanctus

Sanctus, Sanctus, Sanctus, Dominus Deus Sabaoth. Pleni sunt caeli et terra gloria tua. Hosanna in excelsis. Benedictus qui venit in nomine Domini. Hosanna in excelsis.

Holy, holy, holy, Lord God of hosts. The heavens and the earth are full of your glory. Hosanna in the highest. Blessed is He who comes in the name of the Lord. Hosanna in the highest.

plenus – full, *pleni* = plural
gloria tua – Ablative Case of *gloria* – 'of your glory'
in excelsis – Ablative Case plural of *excelsus* – high

Lex Dei – Law of God
Lex Naturalis – Natural Law
Lex Mosaica – Law of Moses
lēx, lēgis, f. (3)

This prayer contains two Hebrew words coming from the Old Testament (***Vetus Testamentum***):
Hosanna – אן העישוה (hosia na) is a request – 'save,' 'help.'
In the New Testament (***Novum Testamentum***) this word is used as an exclamation of celebration.
Sabaoth – צבאות (tsvaot) means 'army' in the Old Testament. As the title of God, it is used speaking of God as the leader of the armies of Israel. Later it came to mean 'heavenly hosts,' or angels, so ***Deus Sabaoth*** is 'the God of the Heavenly Hosts.'

Here are the words the priest says over the Chalice of communion:
Hic est enim calix sanguinis mei, novi et aeterni testamenti: mysterium fidei, qui pro vobis et pro multis effendetur in remissionem peccatorum.
For this is the chalice of my blood of the new and everlasting testament, the mystery of faith, which for you and for many shall be shed unto the remission of sins.

Genitive Case: *sanguinis mei – sanguis meus – sanguis, sanguinis,* m. (3) – blood
novi et aeterni testamenti – Novum et Aeternum Testamentum – testāmentum, testāmentī, n. (2)
fidei – fidēs, fideī, f. (5) – faith • *peccatorum* – Genitive plural of *peccātum, peccātī,* n. (2) – sin
Ablative Case: *pro vobis – vos* – you • *pro multis – multus* – many, numerous

MONTES
SAMARITANUS MISERICORDIA MOTUS EST.
NOX
ASINA
VIA
HOMO VULNERATUS, SEMIVIVO RELICTO

Commemoratio Omnium Fidelium Defunctorum – the Feast of All Souls, November 2

Ave Maria

Ave Maria, gratia plena, Dominus tecum. Benedicta tu in mulieribus, et benedictus fructus ventris tui, Jesus. Sancta Maria, Mater Dei, ora pro nobis peccatoribus, nunc, et in hora mortis nostrae. Amen.

Hail Mary, full of grace, the Lord is with you. Blessed are you among women, and blessed is the fruit of your womb, Jesus. Holy Mary, Mother of God, pray for us, sinners, now, and at the hour of our death. Amen.

FLAGELLUM

VENDENTES BOVES ET OVES ET COLUMBAS

OMNES EIECIT DE TEMPLO.

TEMPLUM

gratia plena – *gratia* is the Ablative case of *gratia, gratiae* f. (1) – grace, good will
in mulieribus – Ablative plural of *mulier, mulieris,* f. (3) – woman
ventris tui – Genitive case of *venter, ventris,* m. (3) – womb, stomach
pro nobis peccatoribus – Ablative case of *nos* – we, and *peccātor, peccātōris,* m. (3) – sinner
in hora – Ablative case of *hōra, hōrae,* f. (1) – hour
mortis nostrae – Genitive case of mors, *mortis,* f. (3) – death

Amen is another word of Hebrew origin – אָמֵן – *amen* is used in the Old Testament as a response word said when hearing a prayer or a blessing.

decalogus – the *Decalogue*, the Ten Commandments

If you don't yet know by heart *Pater Noster* and *Ave Maria*, please put time into learning these prayers. If you remember all the Genitive and Ablative forms listed above, your job is almost done with these two cases. And you will remember that the prepositions *in* and *pro* are used with the Ablative case!

ECCE HOMO.

CANA GALILAEAE

VINUM NON HABENT.

WOW! VINUM BONUM!

AQUA VINUM FACTA EST!

HYDRIAS

LESSON III

Genitive ▬▬▬ Ablative ▬▬▬ Vocative ▬▬▬

Vocative Case

The easiest case in Latin is the **Vocative case**. It's an address form used only when you talk to someone. For most nouns Vocative case = Nominative case. The only big exception is:
The 2nd Declension masculine nouns ending in **- us** change their ending to **- e** in the Vocative case.
For example, as a form of address, *Dominus* turns into *Domine*:
De profundis clamavi ad te, Domine (*Psalmus 129*)...
Out of the depths I have cried to You, O Lord...
Dominus Iesus Christus turns into *Domine Iesu Christe* when you address Jesus in prayer.

Esse

Are you ready to attack Latin verbs? Again, in comparison with English, Latin verbs have a mountain of forms, but that's where learning your Latin prayers by heart comes in handy! Before you know it, you will be able to recite all those verb forms in your sleep!... and, we hope, also when awake! ;)
Take a look at the verbs you already know from the prayers we studied in the previous chapter:
qui es in caelis • *es* = [you] are • *Pleni sunt caeli et terra...* • *sunt* = [they] are
credo = [I] believe • *ora pro nobis* – *ora* = pray (command form/Imperative mood)

So let's get the Latin verb *esse* = 'to be' out of the way first!
Verbs such as 'to be,' 'to want,' 'to eat,' 'to go' are the most ancient, and for that reason they are usually the most irregular in all languages. In English, the verb 'to be' changes its forms quite a bit: am/is/are in the Present tense, was/were in the Past tense.
When verbs change their forms, we call it **conjugation**. Verbs **conjugate**.
Here is a conjugation chart for the verb *esse* in the Present tense:

sum	I am	*sumus*	we are
es	you are	*estis*	you (plural) are
est	he/she/it is	*sunt*	they are

Because this verb changes its forms for the 1st, 2nd, and 3rd persons (I, you, are), and for 2 numbers – singular and plural, you don't even have to use personal pronouns with it! *sum* = I am

It's the same as using 'am' without 'I'. 'Am' is used only with I, so why bother to use 'I' at all?
You can just say 'am' - *sum*!

Vos estis sal terrae... vos estis lux mundi (Matt. 5:13-14)
You are the salt of the earth. You are the light of the world.
...ubi enim est thesaurus tuus, ibi est et cor tuum. (Matt. 6:21)
For where your treasure is, there is your heart also.
Quia tu es, Deus, fortitudo mea... – For you, O God, are my strength...
Quare tristis es, anima mea? – Why are you sad, O my soul?
Gratias agamus Domino Deo nostro. Dignum et iustum est.
Let us give thanks to the Lord our God. It is fitting and just.
Ite, missa est. – Go, the mass is over.

AVE REX IUDAEORUM!

VERE HOMO HIC FILIUS DEI EST!

Verb Conjugations, Present Tense

Verbs are divided into 4 conjugation groups – or **conjugations**. If you know the forms of one verb in each conjugation group, you can easily figure out the forms for any verb in that group. Here is a chart of the Present Tense verb endings:

I	- o	we	- mus
you	- s	you (plural)	- tis
he/she/it	- t	they	- nt

Sacramentum – Sacrament
sacrāmentum, sacrāmentī, n. (2)
ex Opere Operato – 'out of the work worked'
opus, operis, n. (3)
operato – Past Participle, Ablative
operor, operārī, operātum – to work

We've already seen these endings with the verb *esse*. However, verbs of different conjugations have different stems, so even though the endings are the same, you will see different vowels before the ending. Look at the infinitive forms of the verbs below. Their stems end in - *a*, - *e*, - *i*.

amare – to love – 1st conjugation
videre – to see – 2nd conjugation
legere – to read – 3rd conjugation
venire – to come – 4th conjugation

Here is a conjugation chart for these 4 verbs in the Present tense:

Verbum caro factum est et habitavit in nobis.

conjugation:	1	2	3	4
I	amo	video	lego	venio
you	amas	vides	legis	venis
he/she/it	amat	videt	legit	venit
we	amamus	videmus	legimus	venimus
you (plural)	amatis	videtis	legitis	venitis
they	amant	vident	legunt	veniunt

If you remember the Present tense forms for each of these verbs, you will recognize most Present tense verb forms.

Traditionally, the way to learn new verbs in Latin is to memorize four forms for each verb. These forms are called the **principal parts**. They show what conjugation the verb belongs to, and whether it changes its stem across its many forms.

The principal parts of the Latin verb *scribere* – to write – are:

1. *scrībō* – I write – Present tense, 1st person, singular
2. *scrībere* – to write – infinitive
3. *scrīpsī* – I have written – Past Perfect tense, 1st person, singular
4. *scrīptum* – written – Past Participle, neuter, singular

TABERNACULUM

Most dictionaries list these four principal parts for each Latin verb, plus the number of its conjugation, like this:

scrībō, scrībere, scrīpsī, scrīptum (3) – to write
amō, amāre, amāvī, amātum (1) – to love
videō, vidēre, vīdī, vīsum (2) – to see
legō, legere, lēgī, lēctum (3) – to read
veniō, venīre, vēnī, ventum (4) – to come

Laudare, Benedicere, Praedicare
To Praise, To Bless, To Preach
(motto of the Dominican order)
laudare – to praise – 1st conjugation
benedicere – to bless – 3rd conjugation
praedicare – to preach – 1st conjugation

Vestri autem beati oculi quia vident et aures vestrae quia audiunt. (Matt. 13:16)
But blessed are your eyes, for they see, and your ears, for they hear.

Dicit ei Iesus: Ego sum via, et veritas, et vita. Nemo venit ad Patrem nisi per me. (John 14)
Jesus says to him: I am the way, and the truth, and the life. No man comes to the Father, but by me.

dicit – says – *dīcō, dīcere, dīxī, dictum* (3) – to say
venit – comes – *veniō, venīre, vēnī, ventum* (4) – to come

Benedictus qui venit in nomine Domini.
Blessed be he that comes in the name of the Lord.

Extra Ecclesiam Nulla Salus
Outside the Church there is no salvation
ecclesiam – Accusative case

Many church terms come from Latin.

Advent << *advenire* – to approach, arrive • Annunciation << *annuntiare* – to announce
Ascension << *ascendere* – to ascend • covenant << *convenire* – to come together, to agree
celibate << *caelibatus* – unmarried • clerical, clergy << *clericus* – learned man
commandment << *commendare* – to recommend
diocese << *diocesis* – a governor's jurisdiction
sermon << *sermo* – conversation
ablution << *ablutio* – washing, cleansing
absolution << *absolvere* – to set free
abstinence << *abstinere* – to avoid

RESURRECTIO

RESURREXIT TERTIA DIE

Imperative Mood

communio fidelium – community of the faithful
communio sanctorum – communion of the saints

There are three **moods** in Latin –
Indicative – sentences stating facts – *Orat pro nobis.* – 'He/she prays for us.'
Imperative – commands / requests – *Ora pro nobis!* – 'Pray for us!'
Subjunctive – sentences expressing a wish, talking about a possibility or a condition –
Oremus. – 'May we pray / Let us pray!'

In many prayers we find the Imperative mood – command, or request, forms of verbs.
To turn any verb into a command/request, just remove the ending *-re* from the infinitive
of the verb, and you have a command form:

orare >>> ora >>> Ora pro nobis. – Pray for us.
ōrō, ōrāre, ōrāvī, ōrātum (1) – to pray, to speak

imitatio Christi – imitation of Christ

liberare >>> libera >>> Libera nos a malo. – Deliver us from evil. –
līberō, līberāre, līberāvī, līberātum (1) – to free, release
dare >>> da >>> Da nobis... – Give us... – *dō, dare, dedī, datum* (irregular) - to give
intercedere >>> intercede >>> Intercede pro nobis. – Intercede for us.
intercēdō, intercēdere, intercessī, intercessum (3) – to intervene
ostendere >>> ostende >>> Ostende nobis, Domine, misericordiam tuam.
Show us, Lord, your compassion. – *ostendō, ostendere, ostendī, ostentum* (3) – to show
avere >>> ave >>> Ave Maria... Ave regina caelorum! Ave, domina angelorum! –
Hail Mary! Hail Queen of Heavens! Hail Queen of angels! – *aveō, avēre* (2) – to be well
salvere >>> salve >>> Salve Regina, mater misericordiae
Be well/rejoice Queen, mother of compassion – *salveō, salvēre* (2) – to be well
salvare >>> salva >>> Domine, salva nos, perimus. (Matt.8:25) –
Lord, save us, we are perishing. – *salvō, salvāre* (1) – to save
gaudere >>> gaude >>>
Gaude, Virgo Maria. – Rejoice, O Virgin Mary.
gaudeō, gaudēre, gavīsum (2) – to rejoice

> ESTOTE PERFECTI, SICUT ET PATER VESTER CAELESTIS PERFECTUS EST.

Anima Christi, sanctifica me.
Corpus Christi, salva me...
Soul of Christ, sanctify me.
Body of Christ, save me...
sanctificō, sanctificāre, sanctificāvī, sanctificātum (1) – to sanctify

'Sermon on the mount' by Carl Bloch

ESTOTE = ESSE, IMPERATIVE MOOD

For negative commands/requests use **noli/nolite** + the infinitive of the verb.

Et dixit illis angelus: "Nolite timere."
And the angel said unto them, "Fear not."

Dicit ei Jesus: "Noli me tangere, nondum enim ascendi ad Patrem meum... " (John 20:17).
Jesus said to her, "Do not hold on to me, for I have not yet ascended to the Father..."

Nolite dare sanctum canibus, neque mittatis margaritas vestras ante porcos. (Matt. 7:6)
Do not give that which is holy to the dogs, and do not cast your pearls before swine.

'Flight to Egypt' by Fra Angelico

Beatified in 1982, Fra Angelico was a Dominican friar and one of the most illustrious artists of the Italian Renaissance. They said he used to weep while painting the Crucifixion.

[Painting labels: ELONGAVI FUGIENS 7 MANSI INSOLITUDINE. PS. XXXXXV. C — CAELUS — MONTES — ARBOR — SANCTA FAMILIA — VIA — HERBA — SURGE ACCIPE PUERUM 7 MATREM EP̄ 7 FUGE IN EGIPTUM. MACEI. II. C]

IOSEPH ACCEPIT PUERUM ET MATREM EIUS NOCTE ET RECESSIT IN AEGYPTUM.

SURGE, ACCIPE PUERUM ET MATREM EIUS, ET FUGE IN AEGYPTUM.

NON IN PANE SOLO VIVET HOMO, SED IN OMNI VERBO DEI.

creatio ex nihilo – creation out of nothing

DESERTUM

SI FILIUS DEI ES, DIC LAPIDI HUIC UT PANIS FIAT.

'Christ in the desert' by Ivan Kramskoi

Reading

Genitive   Ablative   Vocative

Gloria in excelsis Deo. Et in terra pax hominibus bonae voluntatis.
Glory to God in the highest and on earth peace to people of good will.
excelsus (adjective) – high • ***voluntās, voluntātis***, f. (3) – will
hominibus – Dative case plural - ***homō, hominis***, m. (3)

Laudamus te. Benedícimus te. Adoramus te. Glorificamus te.
Gratias agimus tibi propter magnam gloriam tuam.
We praise you, we bless you, we adore you, we glorify you,
we give you thanks for your great glory...
Present tense, 1st person plural: ***laudamus, benedicamus, glorificamus, agimus***

> ***liber naturae, liber gratiae, liber gloriae*** – the book of nature, grace, glory (three sources of the knowledge of God)

Domine Deus, Rex caelestis, Deus Pater omnipotens. Domine Fili unigenite, Iesu Christe.
Domine Deus, Agnus Dei, Filius Patris.
Lord God, heavenly King, O God, almighty Father. Lord Jesus Christ, Only Begotten Son, Lord God, Lamb of God, Son of the Father...
Vocative case: ***Deus, Dómine Fili unigénite, Iesu Christe...***

Qui tollis peccáta mundi, miserére nobis. Qui tollis peccáta mundi,
súscipe deprecatiónem nostram. Qui sedes ad déxteram Patris, miserére nobis.
You who take away the sins of the world, have mercy on us; who take away the sins of the world, receive our prayer; who are seated at the right hand of the Father, have mercy on us.
Imperative mood:
miserere – ***misereō, miserēre, miseruī, miseritum / misertum*** (2) – to have compassion
suscipe – ***suscipiō, suscipere, suscēpī, susceptum*** (3) – to support
Present tense:
tollis – ***tollō, tollere, sustulī, sublātum*** (irr.) – to lift, to take away
sedes – ***sedeō, sedēre, sēdī, sessum*** (2) – to sit

> ***prima causa*** – the first cause; God as the cause of all things

Quóniam tu solus Sanctus. Tu solus Dóminus. Tu solus Altíssimus,
Iesu Christe. Cum Sancto Spíritu in glória Dei Patris. Amen.
For you alone are the Holy One, you alone are the Lord, you alone are the Most High, Jesus Christ, with the Holy Spirit, in the glory of God the Father. Amen.

LESSON IV

voluntas revelata Dei – the revealed will of God

Just like English, Latin has a few past tenses, or ways to talk about the past.
In English we can say, 'I wrote,' 'I was writing,' 'I have written,' 'I have been writing'...
The helper verb 'have' usually signals that the action is completed.
This type of tense is called **perfect**.
In Latin we also have **perfect** tenses to describe 1-time actions, and
imperfect tenses to describe actions that continue for a while, or are repeated.

Iesus descendit ad inferos, tertia die resurrexit a mortuis, ascendit ad caelos.
Jesus descended into hell, on the third day rose from the dead, [and] ascended into Heaven.
In this sentence the verbs *descendit, resurrexit, ascendit* are 1-time actions that happened
in the past – **Past Perfect tense**.
For actions that continued or were repeated in the past, we would use the **Past Imperfect tense**:
Iesus docebat discipulos. Discipuli orabant.
Jesus taught disciples. Disciples prayed.

Here are the most common endings of Latin verbs for these 2 types of past tense:

Imperfect Past tense endings			**Perfect Past** tense endings:	
I	- bam	ōrābam	- i	ōrāvī
you	- bas	ōrābās	- isti	ōrāvistī
he, she, it	- bat	ōrābat	- it	ōrāvit
we	- bamus	ōrābāmus	- imus	ōrāvimus
you (plural)	- batis	ōrābātis	- istis	ōrāvistis
they	- bant	ōrābant	- erunt	ōrāvērunt

ōrō, ōrāre, ōrāvī, ōrātum (1) - to pray, to talk

Important! In the Past Perfect tense Latin verbs change their stem. That's why a Past Perfect form
is one of the principal parts of the verb: It shows how a verb changes its stem in its Perfect forms.
Some verbs have *v* added to the Past Perfect stem: *orare* = to pray >> *oravi*
Some verbs change *t* in their stem to *s*: *mittere* = to send, *misi*
Some verbs change *c* to *x*: *ducere* = to lead, *duxi*
Some verbs change the vowel at the end of their stem. For example, *videre* switches from *e* to *i*:
video = I see, *vidi* = I saw

In some instances the Present and Past Perfect forms of a verb are distinguished only by the length of the vowel:

venit – he/she/it comes

vēnit – he/she/it came

principio – finis
iustus – peccator
caelus – terra

After Latin stopped being a live conversational language, the difference between the long and short vowels was lost, and some forms can be identified only by context.

As always, irregular verbs go their own way!
Here is a chart of the Past Perfect and Imperfect forms of the verb *esse*.

	Past Imperfect	Past Perfect
I was	eram	fuī
you were	eras	fuisti
he/she/it was	erat	fuit
we were	eramus	fuimus
you (plural) were	eratis	fuistis
they were	erant	fuerunt

Genitive   Ablative

Reading the *Vulgata* you encounter a lot of **Latin Conjunctions** – little words that connect phrases, or sentences. They include:

aut – or
neque – nor
igitur – therefore
sicut – just as
etiam, quoque – also
sed, autem, vero – but
quia, quod, quoniam – because
enim – for
iam – now, already
quamquam – although

Stabat mater dolorosa iuxta crucem lacrymosa
Dum pendebat filius...

Imperfect Past tense:

stabat – *stō, stāre, stetī, statum* (1) – to stand

pendebat – *pendō, pendere, pependī, pēnsum* (3) – to hang

Petrus autem et Johannes ascendebant in templum ad horam orationis nonam. (Acts 3:1)

But Peter and John used to go up to the temple at the hour of prayer, the ninth hour.

Non veni vocare iustos, sed peccatores in paenitentiam. (Luke 5:32)

I came not to call the righteous, but sinners to repentance.

Present tense = *venio*; Past Perfect tense = *veni*

In principio creavit Deus caelum et terram. >> *creō, creāre, creāvī, creātum* (1) – to create

Domus Israel speravit in Domino. >> *spērō, spērāre, spērāvī, spērātum* (1) – to hope

Et Verbum caro factum est, et habitavit in nobis, et vidimus gloriam eius...

And the Word was made flesh, and lived among us, and we saw His glory...

habitavit – Past Perfect tense of *habitō, habitāre, habitāvī, habitātum* (1) – to live, to inhabit

vidimus – Past Perfect tense of *videō, vidēre, vīdī, vīsum* (2) – to see

Beati qui non viderunt,
Et firmiter crediderunt.
Vitam aeternam habebunt.
Alleluia.

RELIQUIÆ SĀNCTŌRUM

Past Perfect tense:

viderunt – *videō, vidēre, vīdī, vīsum* (2) – to see
crediderunt – *crēdō, crēdere, crēdidī, crēditum* (3) – to believe

Future Imperfect tense:

habebunt – *habeō, habēre, habuī, habitum* (2) – to have

Et duxit illum diabolus et ostendit illi omnia regna orbis terrae in momento temporis. (Luke 4:5)
And the devil, taking him up into a high mountain, showed unto him all the kingdoms of the world in a moment of time.

Et duxit illum in Hierusalem et statuit eum supra pinnam templi et dixit illi:
'Si Filius Dei es, mitte te hinc deorsum.' (Luke 4:9)
And he brought him to Jerusalem, and set him on a pinnacle of the temple, and said unto him, If you are the Son of God, cast yourself down from here.

Quando Thomas vidit Christum,
Pedes, manus, latus suum,
Dixit : Tu es Deus meus. Alleluia.

Past Perfect tense:

vidit – *videō, vidēre, vīdī, vīsum* (2) – to see
dixit – *dīcō, dīcere, dīxī, dictum* (3) – to say
Christum – Accusative case of *Christus*
pedes – *pēs, pedis,* m. (3) – foot – plural Accusative: *pedes*
manus – *manus, manūs,* f. (4) – plural Accusative: *manus*
latus suum – singular Accusative of
latus suus – *latus, lateris,* n. (3) – side

EMMAUS

ET APERTI SUNT OCULI EORUM ET COGNOVERUNT EUM.

NONNE COR NOSTRUM ARDENS ERAT IN NOBIS?

IESUS IN MEDIO DOCTORUM AUDIT ILLOS ET INTERROGAT.

TEMPLUM

DOCTORES

STUPEBANT OMNES, QUI EUM AUDIEBANT, SUPER PRUDENTIA ET RESPONSIS EIUS.

Aleluia is another Hebrew word coming from the Old Testament of the Bible.
הַלְלוּיָהּ – hallelu jah – means 'praise God.'

Reading

Genitive – ━━━━━ Ablative – ━━━━━ Vocative ━━━━━

Gloria tibi Domine.

In principio erat Verbum, et Verbum erat apud Deum, et Deus erat Verbum. Hoc erat in principio apud Deum. Omnia per ipsum facta sunt: et sine ipso factum est nihil, quod factum est. In ipso vita erat, et vita erat lux hominum: et lux in tenebris lucet, et tenebrae eam non comprehenderunt. Fuit homo missus a Deo, cui nomen erat Ioannes. Hic venit in testimonium ut testimonium perhiberet de lumine, ut omnes crederent per illum. Non erat ille lux, sed ut testimonium perhiberet de lumine. Erat lux vera, quae illuminat omnem hominem venientem in hunc mundum. In mundo erat, et mundus per ipsum factus est, et mundus eum non cognovit. In propria venit, et sui eum non receperunt. Quodquot autem receperunt eum, dedit eis potestatem filios Dei fieri, his qui credunt in nomine eius: qui non ex sanguinibus, neque ex voluntate carnis, neque ex voluntate viri, sed ex Deo nati sunt. Et verbum caro factum est, et habitavit in nobis: et vidimus gloriam eius, gloriam quasi unigeniti a Patre plenum gratiae et veritatis. Deo gratias.

Present tense:

lucet – lūceō, lūcēre, lūxī (2) – to shine

illuminat – illūminō, illūmināre, illūmināvī, illūminātum (1) – to illuminate

credunt – crēdō, crēdere, crēdidī, crēditum (3) – to believe

> *verus – falsus*
> *spiritus – caro*
> *natus – creatus*

Past Perfect:

comprehenderunt – comprehendō, comprehendere, comprehendī, comprehēnsum (3) – to grasp

venit – veniō, venīre, vēnī, ventum (4)

cognovit – cōgnōscō, cōgnōscere, cōgnōvī, cōgnitum (3) – to recognize

receperunt – recipiō, recipere, recēpī, receptum (3) – to receive

dedit – dō, dare, dedī, datum (irr.) – to give

habitavit – habitō, habitāre, habitāvī, habitātum (1) – to live

vidimus – videō, vidēre, vīdī, vīsum (2)

Infinitive: *fieri – fīō, fierī, factum* – to happen, to take place

> *lux, lumen – tenebrae*
> *omnia – nihil*
> *dare – recipere*
> *illuminare – obscurare*
> *credere – dubitare*

Past Participles:

facta sunt, factus est, factum est – of *faciō, facere, fēcī, factum* (3) – to do, to make

missus – Past Participle of *mittō, mittere, mīsī, missum* (3) - to send

Subjunctive mood:

ut perhiberet – 'so that he presents' – *perhibeō, perhibēre, perhibuī, perhibitum* (2) – to present

ut crederent – 'so that they believe' – *crēdō, crēdere, crēdidī, crēditum* (3)

'Baptism of Christ'
by Fra Angelico

IOHANNES BAPTISTA PRAEDICAT IN DESERTO IUDAEAE.

ECCE APERTI SUNT CAELI!

SPIRITUS SANCTUS

HIC EST FILIUS MEUS DILECTUS.

MONTES APUD IORDANEN

VOX CLAMANTIS IN DESERTO

MONS ALTUS

EGO A TE DEBEO BAPTIZARI, ET TU VENIS AD ME?

ECCLESIA

IORDAN FLUMEN

PORTAE

AQUA

FORUM

VESTIMENTUM DE PILIS CAMELORUM

CIVITAS

IOHANNES BAPTISTA

ANGELI DEI

CHRISTUS

Glory be to You, O Lord.

In the beginning was the word, and the word was with God, and God was the word. This was in the beginning with God. All things were made by him: and without him was made nothing, which was made. In him was life, and the life was the light of men: and the light shines in darkness, and the darkness did not comprehend it. There was a man sent from God, whose name was John. This man came for testimony, to give testimony of the light, that all might believe through him. He was not the light: but to give testimony of the light. It was the true light, which lightens every man that comes into this world. He was in the world, and the world was made by him, and the world knew him not. He came into his own, and his own received him not. But as many as received him, he gave them power to be made the sons of God, to those that believe in his name. Who, not of blood nor of the will of flesh, nor of the will of man, but of God are born. And the word was made flesh, and dwelt in us, and we saw the glory of him, glory as it were of the only begotten of the Father, full of grace and verity. Thanks be to God.

Lesson V

Back to nouns! In this class we'll study the Accusative and the Dative cases.
On the following page is a chart of Latin noun endings for all cases, all five declensions.

Accusative Case

The Accusative case is most commonly used with a direct object – a thing produced by an action ('to bake a cake') or an effect of an action ('to negotiate peace').
Ego autem dico vobis diligite inimicos vestros... (Matt. 5:44)
But I say unto you, love your enemies...
In the declension chart notice that the Nominative and Accusative case forms of neuter nouns – singular and plural – coincide.
Agnus Dei, qui tollis peccata mundi, miserere nobis... dona nobis pacem.
Lamb of God, Who takes away the sins of the world: have mercy on us... grant us peace.
peccata – plural Accusative case = Plural Nominative case of *peccātum, peccātī,* n – sin
pacem – Accusative case of *pāx, pācis,* f – peace

In the Accusative case past participles and most adjectives echo the noun endings.
singular: m. *- um*, f. *- am*, n. *- um*
plural: m. *- os*, f. *- as*, n. *- a*
iudicare vivos et mortuos – to judge the living and the dead

Genitive   Ablative   Accusative

Gratia non tollit naturam, sed perficit.
Grace does not take away nature, but perfects it (St. Thomas Aquinas, *Summa Theologiae I*)
Adeste Fideles, laeti triumphantes,
Venite, venite in Bethlehem.
Natum videte regem angelorum,
Venite adoremus, venite adoremus,
Venite adoremus, Dominum.
regem – Accusative case of *rēx, rēgis,* m – king • *gnāscor, gnāscī, nātum* – to be born
natum – Accusative case of *natus*, past participle formed from the verb
dominum – Accusative case of *dominus, dominī,* m. (2) – lord
Imperative Mood, 2nd person plural: *adeste, venite, videte*

NOUN ENDINGS IN 5 DECLENSIONS

DECL.	1	2		3		4		5
GENDER	F.	M.	N.	M./F.	N.	M.	N.	F.
SINGULAR								
NOM.	- a	- us	- um	- s (modified stem)		- us	- ū	- ēs
GEN.	- ae	- ī	- ī	- is	- is	- ūs	- ūs	- ēī / e
DAT.	- ae	- ō	- ō	- ī	- ī	- uī /ū	=Nom.	- ēī / e
ACC.	- am	- um	=Nom.	- em/im	=Nom.	- um	=Nom.	- em
ABL.	- ā	- ō	- ō	- e/ī	- e/ī	- ū	=Nom.	- ē
VOC.	=Nom.	- e	=Nom.	=Nom.	=Nom.	=Nom.	=Nom.	=Nom.
PLURAL								
NOM.	- ae	- ī	- a	- ēs	- a, - ia	- ūs	- ua	- ēs
GEN.	- ārum	- ōrum	- ōrum	- um/ium	- um/ium	- uum	- uum	- ērum
DAT.	- īs	- īs	- īs	- ibus	- ibus	- ibus/ubus	- ibus/ubus	- ēbus
ACC.	- ās	- ōs	- a	- ēs (- īs)	- a, - ia	- ūs	- ua	- ēs
ABL.	=Dat.	=Dat.		=Dat.		=Dat.		=Dat.
VOC.	=Nom.	=Nom.		=Nom.		=Nom.		=Nom.

VERB ENDINGS

	PRESENT	PAST / PERFECT	PAST / IMPERFECT	FUTURE / IMPERFECT	
				1,2 conj.	3,4 conj.
I	- ō	- ī	- ba-m	- b-ō	- a-m
you	- s	- is-tī	- bā-s	- bi-s	- ē-s
he, she, it	- t	- i-t	- ba-t	- bi-t	- e-t
we	- mus	- i-mus	- bā-mus	- bi-mus	- ē-mus
you pl.	- tis	- is-tis	- bā-tis	- bi-tis	- ē-tis
they	- nt	- ēru-nt (-ēre)	- ba-nt	- bu-nt	- e-nt

Sinite parvulos venire ad me, et nolite prohibere eos, talium est enim regnum caelorum, et Angeli eorum semper vident faciem Patris Mei... (Matt.19:14)

Allow the little children to come to Me, and forbid them not, for of such is the kingdom of heaven, and their angels always behold the face of My Father...

parvus – little

faciēs, faciēī, f. (5) – face, appearance

talis – such

Imperative mood:

sinite – sinō, sinere, sīvī, situm (3) – allow

nolite prohibere – prohibeō, prohibēre, prohibuī, prohibitum (2) – to prevent

'Temptation on the Mount' by Duccio di Buoninsegna, 1308

Many Latin prepositions are used with the Accusative case, including:

ad – to, toward >> *dixit Maria ad angelum* – Mary said to the angel
ad orientem – to the East – *oriēns, orientis*, m. (3) – sunrise, East
Et creavit Deus hominem ad imaginem suam ad imaginem Dei creavit illum masculum et feminam creavit eos.
So God created human beings in his own image, in the image of God he created them; male and female he created them.   *imāgō, imāginis,* f. (3) – image
ante – before >> *ante Deum* – before God
apud – near >> *Verbum erat apud Deum* – the Word was with God
Apud homines hoc impossibile est: apud Deum autem omnia possibilia sunt. (Matt. 19:26)
With man this is impossible, but with God all things are possible.
contra – against >> *Contra verbosos noli contendere verbis.*
Against wordy people don't argue with words. (*Disticha Catonis*)

A.M. – *ante meridiem*
P.M. – *post meridiem*

inter – among, between >> *inter nos* – between us
per – through >> *per Christum Dominum nostrum* – through Christ our Lord;
per omnia saecula saeculorum – through/by ages of ages ('world without end')
Adjuro te per Deum vivum. (Matt. 26:63)
I charge you under oath by the living God.
Ego autem dico vobis non iurare omnino neque per caelum quia thronus Dei est neque per terram... (Matt. 5:35)
But I say unto you, Swear not at all; neither by heaven; for it is God's throne, nor by earth...
post – behind
secundum – following, according to >> *Evangelium Secundum Matthaeum* – Gospel According to Matthew • *Nunc dimittis servum tuum, Domine, secundum verbum tuum in pace...*
Now dismiss Thy servant, O Lord, in peace, according to your word...
propter – because of >>
Sabbatum propter hominem factum est, et non homo propter sabbatum. (Mark 2:27)
The Sabbath was made for man, not man for the Sabbath.
Nolite iudicare secundum faciem, sed iustum iudicium iudicate. (John 7:24)
Do not judge after the appearance, but judge a righteous judgment.
faciem – *faciēs, faciēī,* f. (5) – face • *iustum iudicium* – from *iustus iudicium*
iūdicium, iūdiciī, n. (2) – judgement

The preposition *in* is used
- with the Ablative case when it indicates location – in, inside, among –
- with the Accusative case when speaking about movement – into.

Et ne nos inducas in tentationem... – And lead us not into temptation...

Because 'leading' implies movement, *in tentationem* is an Accusative case form.

Ego quidem baptizo vos in aqua in poenitentiam. (Matt. 3:11)

I baptize you with [in] water for repentance.

SACERDOS

SPONSUS   SPONSA

MATRIMONIUM

BENEDIC, DOMINE, ANULUM HUNC.

In the Rite of Marriage *in* + Accusative signals a change of status – from unmarried to married.

– ***Vis accípere [nomen] hic praesentem in tuam legítimam uxórem juxta ritum sanctae matris Ecclésiae?***

Do you want to take [name] here present, for your lawful wife according to the rite of our holy mother, the Church?

– ***Volo.*** – I want.

– ***Vis accípere [nomen] hic praesentem in tuum legítimum marítum juxta ritum sanctae matris Ecclésiae?***

Do you want to take [name] here present, for your lawful husband according to the rite of our holy mother, the Church?

– ***Volo.*** – I want.

uxor, uxōris, f (3) – wife • marītus, marītī, m (2) – husband

juxta ritum – rītus, rītūs, m (4) – rite

Accusative case is also used with the verb *credere* = to believe in/into. Let us read

Symbolum Apostolorum – the *Apostles' Creed* – and notice the use of the preposition *in*.

Credo in Deum Patrem omnipotentem, Creatorem caeli et terrae

I believe in God, the Father almighty, Creator of Heaven and earth

Et in Iesum Christum, Filium eius unicum, Dominum nostrum

and in Jesus Christ, His only Son, our Lord

qui conceptus est de Spiritu Sancto, natus ex Maria Virgine, passus sub Pontio Pilato

who was conceived by the Holy Ghost, born of the Virgin Mary, suffered under Pontius Pilate

crucifixus, mortuus, et sepultus, descendit ad inferos, tertia die resurrexit a mortuis, ascendit ad caelos

[who] was crucified, died, was buried, descended into hell, on the third day rose from the dead, [and] ascended into Heaven

Past Perfect:

descendit – dēscendō, dēscendere, dēscendī, dēscēnsum (3) – to descend
resurrexit – resurgō, resurgere, resurrēxī, resurrēctum (3) – to rise again
ascendit – ascendō, ascendere, ascendī, ascēnsum (3) – to ascend
sedet ad dexteram Dei Patris omnipotentis, inde venturus est iudicare vivos et mortuos.
[who] sits at the right hand of God the Father Almighty, from there [He] will come
to judge the living and the dead.
dextera, dexterae, f. (1) – right hand
Credo in Spiritum Sanctum, sanctam Ecclesiam Catholicam, sanctorum communionem, remissionem peccatorum, carnis resurrectionem, vitam aeternam. Amen.
I believe in the Holy Spirit, the Holy Catholic Church, the communion of saints,
the forgiveness of sins, the resurrection of the body, life everlasting. Amen.
commūniō, commūniōnis, f. (3) – communion
remissiō, remissiōnis, f. (3) – release
resurrectiō, resurrectiōnis, f. (3) – resurrection
sānctus, sānctī, m. (2) – saint • *peccātum, peccātī,* n. (2) – sin • *carō, carnis,* f. (3) – flesh

Personal pronouns in the Accusative case are:

ego	me
tu	te
is, ea, id	eum, eam, id
nos	nos
vos	vos
ei, eae, ea	eos, eas, ea

Qui videt me, videt eum qui misit me. (John 12:45)
He who sees me, sees him who sent me.

Es, Domine, mecum, te rogo.
Be with me, Lord, I ask you.

A special use of the Accusative case is the **Accusativus cum Infinitivo** construction.
In a sentence like 'I believe you to be the Son of God,'
'you' in Latin would be in Accusative Case. In Matt. 16:15 Jesus asks his disciples:
Quem me esse dicitis? – Who do you say I am? • **quem** is the Accusative case of **quis**,
so a literal translation of this question would be: "Whom do you say me to be?"
Accusativus cum Infinitivo was very widely used in Classical Latin with words like 'say,'
'believe,' 'think,' 'consider,' 'guess,' and so on. In *Vulgata*, however, this construction
is not very common.
His autem, qui matrimonio iuncti sunt, praecipio, non ego sed Dominus, uxorem a viro non discedere. (1 Cor. 7:10) – And unto the married I command, yet not I, but the Lord,
for the wife not to depart from her husband.

"Lazarus" by Fra Angelico

Reading

Prayer Before Meals

Benedic, Domine, nos et haec tua dona quae de tua largitate sumus sumpturi.
Per Christum Dominum nostrum. Amen.

Bless us, O Lord, and these Thy gifts which we are about to receive from Thy bounty through Christ, Our Lord, amen.

dōnum, dōnī, n. (2) – gift

largitās, largitātis, f. (3) – abundance, generosity

sumus sumpturi – Future tense participle – 'are to be receiving'

sūmō, sūmere, sūmpsī, sūmptum (3) – to take, to choose

benedic – Imperative mood

Habemus papam! – We have a pope!

Pope Pius IX

Prayer After Meals

Agimus tibi gratias, omnipotens Deus, pro universis beneficiis tuis, qui vivis et regnas in saecula saeculorum. Fidelium animae, per misericordiam Dei, requiescant in pace. Amen.

We give You thanks for all Your benefits, O Almighty God, Who lives and reigns forever. And may the souls of the faithful departed, through the mercy of God, rest in peace. Amen.

beneficium, beneficiī, n. (2) – benefit, kindness
saēculum, saēculī, n. (2) – age
misericordia, misericordiae, f. (1) – compassion
fidelis – faithful

vir – mulier, femina
puer, adolescens – puella, virgo

Et cum venisset Iesus in domum principis et vidisset tibicines et turbam tumultuantem, dicebat: "Recedite! Non est enim mortua puella, sed dormit."
Et deridebant eum. Et cum eiecta esset turba intravit et tenuit manum eius, et surrexit puella.
Et exiit fama haec in universam terram illam. (Matt 9:23)

Past Perfect:
intravit – *intrō, intrāre, intrāvī, intrātum* (1) – to enter
tenuit – *teneō, tenēre, tenuī, tentum* (2) – to hold
surrexit – *surrigō, surrigere, surrēxī, surrēctum* (3) – to rise
exiit – *exeō, exīre, exiī / exivī, exitum* (irr.) – to exit

Past Imperfect:
dicebat – *dīcō, dīcere, dīxī, dictum* (3) – to say
deridebant – *dērīdeō, dērīdēre, dērīsī, dērīsum* (2) – to laugh at
venisset, vidisset – 'when he came, saw...' – Subjunctive Pluperfect
esset – Subjunctive Imperfect – *sum, esse, fuī, futūrum* (irr.) – to be

And when Jesus came into the ruler's house, and saw the mourners and the crowd making noise, He said unto them, "Step aside. The girl is not dead, but is sleeping." And they laughed at him. But when the people were moved out of the way, he went in, and took her by the hand, and the girl arose. And the news of that spread over that whole land.

BIBLIA SACRA

BENEDICTUS QUI TOLLIT CRUCEM.

ET BAIULANS SIBI CRUCEM, EXIVIT IN EUM QUI DICITUR CALVARIAE LOCUM.

MILITES ROMANI

Lesson VI

PULVIS ES ET IN PULVEREM REVERTERIS.

Dative Case

Our last case is **Dative**. Its most common use is indirect object. 'Give it to me.' – 'to me' is the Dative case in Latin.

Genitive   Ablative   Accusative   Dative

Let's go back to the Lord's Prayer and read it, noticing the use of the Dative and other cases.
Pater noster, qui es in caelis, sanctificetur nomen tuum. Adveniat regnum tuum.
Fiat voluntas tua, sicut in caelo et in terra. Panem nostrum quotidianum da nobis hodie,
et dimitte nobis debita nostra sicut et nos dimittimus debitoribus nostris.
Et ne nos inducas in tentationem, sed libera nos a malo. Amen.
dēmittō, dēmittere, dēmīsī, dēmissum (3) – to drop, to let go
dēbitor, dēbitōris, m. (3) – debtor • *pānis, pānis*, m. (3) – bread
dēbitum, dēbitī, n. (2) – debt
tentātiō, tentātiōnis, f. (3) – temptation
malum, malī, n. (2) – evil

A special use of the Dative case is Dative + *esse* to indicate belonging / possession:
Quod tibi nomen est? – What is your name?
Argentum et aurum non est mihi. (Acts 3:6)
Silver and gold have I none.

VIR DIVES

VIDUA

OMNIA QUAE HABUIT MISIT

DIVITES IACTABANT MULTA, VIDUA PAUPER MISIT DUO MINUTA.

Notice the use of Dative case pronouns and nouns in the following passages.
Deo Optimo Maximo (D.O.M.)
For God, the best and greatest (motto of the Benedictines)
Gloria Patri, et Filio, et Spiritui Sancto. Sicut erat in principio,
et nunc, et semper, et in saecula saeculorum. Amen.
Glory be to the Father, and to the Son, and to the Holy Spirit. As it was in the beginning, is now, and ever shall be, world without end. Amen.
Gloria in excelsis Deo. Et in terra pax hominibus bonae voluntatis.
Glory to God in the highest. And on Earth peace to people of good will.
homō, hominis, m. (3) – man
voluntās, voluntātis, f. (3) – will

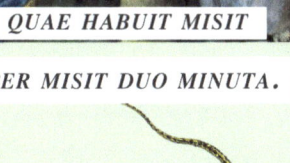

SERPENS

Gratias agamus Domino Deo nostro. Dignum et iustum est.
Let us give thanks to the Lord our God. It is appropriate and just.

Pax huic domui. Et omnibus habitantibus in ea.
Peace be unto this house. And unto all who dwell therein.
huic domui – from **haec domus** – **domus, domūs / -ī**, f. (4, 2) – house
omnibus habitantibus – Dative Case plural of **omnes habitantes** – all living

gaudere	– to feel joy
gaudens	– joyful
laetari	– to express joy
laetus	– expressing joy

Quid mihi prodest, si mortui non resurgunt? (1 Cor. 15:32)
What does it profit me if the dead rise not?
mihi – Dative case of **ego** = I

Et ecce aperti sunt ei caeli.... (Matt. 3:16)
And behold the heavens were opened for him...
ei – Dative case of **is** = he

Personal Pronouns

Nominative	Dative
ego	mihi
tu	tibi
is, ea, id	ei
nos	nobis
vos	vobis
ei, eae, ea	eis

Non nobis, Domine, non nobis: sed nomini tuo da gloriam.
Not unto us, O Lord, not unto us: but unto Thy name give the glory.
Dative case:
nōmen, nōminis, n. (3) – name

Disticha Catonis

Disticha Catonis or the *Distichs of Cato* are 2-line wisdom sayings collected by Dionysius Cato in the 3-4th century AD. The *Disticha Catonis* collection was used as a Latin textbook in Europe from the Middle Ages through the 18th century.

Cum te aliquis laudat, iudex tuus esse memento;
Plus aliis de te, quam tu tibi, credere noli.
(from *Disticha Catonis*)
When someone praises you, remember to be your own judge;
Do not believe others about you more, than you believe yourself.
aliis – plural Dative – **alius** = another
memento is a command/request form of
meminī, meminisse, meminī (3) – to remember

Proximus ille Deo est, qui scit ratione tacere.
(from *Disticha Catonis*)
He is close to God who knows
how to keep quiet properly.

NOE DIMISIT COLUMBAM EX ARCA.

COLUMBA VENIT PORTANS RAMUM OLIVAE.

Declension of Latin Pronouns

SINGULAR				M.	F.	N.	
NOM.	egō	tū		is	ea	id	
GEN.	meī	tuī		eius	eius	eius	suī
DAT.	mihī	tibi		ei	ei	ei	sibi
ACC.	mē	tē		eum	eam	id	sē / sēsē
ABL.	mē	tē		eo	ea	eo	sē / sēsē

PLURAL				M.	F.	N.	
NOM.	nōs	vōs		ei	eae	ea	
GEN.	nostrī /nostrum	vestrī / vestrum		eorum	earum	eorum	suī
DAT.	nōbīs	vōbīs		eis	eis	eis	sibi
ACC.	nōs	vōs		eos	eas	ea	sē / sēsē
ABL.	nōbīs	vōbīs		eis	eis	eis	sē / sēsē

SINGULAR	M.	F.	N.	M.	F.	N.	M.	F.	N.
NOM.	hic	haec	hoc	ille	illa	illud	qui	quae	quod
GEN.	huius	huius	huius	illius	illius	illius	cuius	cuius	cuius
DAT.	huic	huic	huic	illi	illi	illi	cui	cui	cui
ACC.	hunc	hanc	hoc	illum	illam	illud	quem	quam	quod
ABL.	hoc	hac	hoc	illo	illa	illo	quo	qua	quo

PLURAL	M.	F.	N.	M.	F.	N.	M.	F.	N.
NOM.	hi	hae	haec	illi	illae	illae	qui	quae	quae
GEN.	horum	harum	horum	illorum	illarum	illorum	quorum	quarum	quorum
DAT.	his	his	his	illis	illis	illis	quibus	quibus	quibus
ACC.	hos	has	haec	illos	illas	illa	quos	quas	quae
ABL.	his	his	his	illis	illis	illis	quibus	quibus	quibus

Latin pronouns decline just like nouns and adjectives, using the same endings.

Pronouns like 'himself,' 'herself,' 'ourselves' are called **Reflexive Pronouns.** As in English, Latin reflexive pronouns *se / suus* replace personal pronouns if they refer to a person who is the subject of the sentence: 'She saw herself in the mirror.'

In propria venit, et sui eum non receperunt.
He came to his own, and his own received him not.

Pronouns *ille, ipse, iste* and *hic* – this / that – are all used as personal pronouns in the *Vulgata*.
hic, haec, hoc – this – denotes objects near to the speaker
ille, illa, illud – that – denotes objects that are more remote
iste, ista, istud – your own – denotes objects that belong to the person you are speaking to
idem, eadem, idem = 'the same.'
ipse, ipsa, ipsum = himself, herself, itself; these pronouns are also used when speaking of famous or divine persons, 'Caesar himself,' 'Christ Himself'
qui, quae, quod – who/what – are interrogative/relative pronouns

Omnia per ipsum facta sunt. (John 1:3)
All things were made through him.

Johannes testimonium perhibet de ipso. (John 1:15)
John bears witness about him.

Ego scio eum, quia ab ipso sum, et ipse misit me. (John 7:29)
I know him, because I am from him, and he sent me.

Vos ascendite ad diem festum hunc: ego non ascendo ad diem festum istum. (John 7:8)
Go up to this feast: I don't go to your feast.

Per ipsum, et cum ipso, et in ipso, est tibi Deo Patri omnipotenti, in unitate Spiritus Sancti, omnis honor et gloria.
Through Him, and with Him, and in Him, is unto Thee, God the Father, Amighty, in the unity of the Holy Ghost, all honor and glory.

dominica – Sunday
Dominica Ressurectionis – Easter Sunday

"ARCUM MEUM PONAM IN NUBIBUS ET ERIT SIGNUM FOEDERIS INTER ME ET INTER TERRAM."

arcus – bow
arca – box

ARCA TESTAMENTI

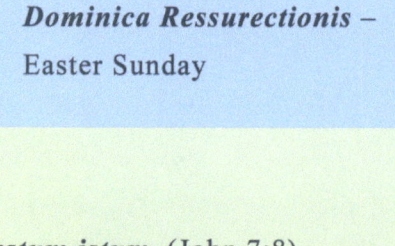

'Christ rescues St. Peter' by Lorenzo Veneziano, 1370

Participles

Latin participles are verbal forms that behave like adjectives. Features that distinguish them from adjectives are: They have tense – present, past, and future – and they can be active or passive, just like verbs. The present and future participles are active and the past/perfect participle is passive.

What are active voice and passive voice in grammar?
active voice: 'I see,' 'I was reading,' 'He will know'
passive voice: 'I am seen,' 'It was read,' 'It will be known'...

IESUS LAVAT PEDES DISCIPULORUM.

salvō, salvāre, salvāvī, salvātum (1) – to save
Action in progress: Present participle, active – **salvans** – saving
Action completed: Past participle, passive – **salvatus** – is/was saved
Action to take place in the future, active: Future participle – **salvaturus** – am/are/is going to save

Future and past participles are mostly used as part of a predicate:

... *venturus est iudicare vivos et mortuos*...
**Tu es qui venturus es,
an alium expectamus?** (Matt.11:3)
Are you he that should come,
or are we to look for another?

HABEMUS QUINQUE PANES ET DUOS PISCES...

ADFERTE ILLOS MIHI.

ET MANDUCAVERUNT OMNES ET SATURATI SUNT.

Participles	Masculine/Feminine		Neuter	
	Singular	Plural	Singular	Plural
Nominative	-ns	-ntes	-ns	-ntia
Genitive	-ntis	-ntium	-ntis	-ntium
Dative	-nti	-ntibus	-nti	-ntibus
Accusative	-ntem	-ntes	-ns	-ntia
Ablative	-nti	-ntibus	-nti	-ntibus

To form a present participle, drop the *-re* infinitive ending, and add case endings from the chart above.

habere >> *habe + ns = habens* – having • *amare* >> *ama + ns = amans* – loving

For verbs of the 4th conjugation you will need to add an *-e* to the stem before the ending.

servire >> *servi + e + ns = serviens* – serving

Euntes ergo docete omnes gentes baptizantes eos in nomine Patris et Filii et Spiritus Sancti.
(Matt.28:19) Go you therefore, and teach all nations, baptizing them in the name of the Father, and of the Son, and of the Holy Spirit.

Present participles:

celebrans – the celebrant

euntes – plural; *iēns* – singular – *eō, īre, itum* (irr.) – to go

baptizantes – plural; *baptīzāns* – singular – *baptīzō, baptīzāre, baptīzāvī, baptīzātum* (1)

Erat lux vera quae illuminat omnem hominem venientem in mundum…(John 1:9)

There was true light that gives light to everyone coming into the world…

Present participle: *venientem* << *veniens* – *veniō, venīre, vēnī, ventum* (4) – to come

Benedicite maledicentibus vobis, orate pro calumniantibus vos. (Luke 6:28)

Bless them that curse you, and pray for them which despitefully use you.

Present participles:

episcopus – bishop

maledicentibus – plural, Dative; *maledicens* – singular –

maledīcō, maledīcere, maledīxī, maledictum (3) – to slander, to abuse

calumniantibus – plural, Dative; *calumnians* – singular –

calumnior, calumniārī, calumniātum (dep.) – accuse falsely

Since *Vulgata* is not an original Latin-language document, but a translation, it has many grammatical features that echo the grammar of the Greek and Hebrew original texts of the Bible. In classical Latin, the verbs *benedicere* and *maledicere* take Accusative Case.
In *Vulgata*, however, they are almost always used with Dative case.

Past participle (singular, neuter) is one of the four principal parts of the verb usually listed in dictionaries: *amo, amare, amavi, amatum* >> *amatum* = past participle

Past participles decline similar to the 1st and 2nd Declension adjectives.

Endings of the 1st and 2nd Declension adjectives, past and future participles

	Singular			Plural		
	Masculine	Feminine	Neuter	Masculine	Femine	Neuter
Nominative	-us	-a	-um	-i	-e	-a
Genitive	-i	-e	-i	-orum	-arum	-orum
Dative	-o	-e	-o	-is	-is	-is
Accusative	-um	-am	-um	-os	-as	-a
Ablative	-o	-a	-o	-is	-is	-is

Gratia enim estis salvati, per fidem, et hoc non ex vobis, Dei enim donum est. (Eph. 2:8)
For it is by grace you have been saved, through faith – and this is not from yourselves, it is the gift of God. Past participle: *estis salvati*

Et respondens angelus dixit ei: 'Ego sum Gabrihel qui adsto ante Deum et missus sum loqui ad te et haec tibi evangelizare.' (Luke 1:19)
And the angel answering said to him, 'I am Gabriel, that stand in the presence of God, and am sent to speak to you, and to bring you good news.'

Present participle: *respondens – respondeō, respondēre, respondī, respōnsum* (2) – to answer
Past participle: *missus sum – mittō, mittere, mīsī, missum* (3) – to send

Vocatum est nomen eius Iesus – his name was called Iesus. (Luke 2:21)
Past participle: *vocatum – vocō, vocāre, vocāvī, vocātum* (1) – to call

Amen dico vobis quia nemo propheta acceptus est in patria sua. (Luke 4:24)
Verily I say unto you, no prophet is accepted in his own country.
Past participle: *acceptus – accipiō, accipere, accēpī, acceptum* (3) – to accept

To form a future participle, replace *m* with *r* in the past participle. Decline it as an adjective.
amatum >> *amaturus, amaturum, amatura* – about to fall in love
habitum >> *habiturus, habitura, habiturum* – about to/intending to have
servitum >> *serviturus, servitura, serviturum* – about to/intending to serve

...omnes homines resurgere habent cum corporibus suis, et reddituri sunt de facti propriis
...all men must arise again with their bodies, and must give an account of their own works
Future participle: *reddituri sunt – redeō, redīre, rediī / redivī, reditum* – to go back

Reading

...secuti sunt eum duo caeci clamantes et dicentes: "Miserere nostri, Fili David!"
Cum autem venisset domum, accesserunt ad eum caeci,
et dicit eis Iesus: "Creditis quia possum hoc facere vobis?"
Dicunt ei: "Utique, Domine."
Tunc tetigit oculos eorum, dicens: "Secundum fidem vestram fiat vobis."
Et aperti sunt oculi illorum, et comminatus est illis Iesus dicens: "Videte ne quis sciat!"
Illi autem exeuntes, diffamaverunt eum in tota terra illa. (Matt 9:27-31)

Present participles: *clamantes, dicentes, dicens*
Past participle: *aperti* – plural – *aperiō, aperīre, aperuī, apertum* (4) – to open
Present tense: *dicit, dicunt, creditis*
Past Perfect: *accesserunt – accēdō, accēdere, accessī, accessum* (3) – to approach
tetigit – tangō, tangere, tetigī, tāctum (3) – to touch
comminatus est – comminor, comminārī, comminātum (deponent verb) – to demand, to order
Present subjunctive:
fiat – 'may it be' – *fīō, fierī, factum* (dep.) – to happen, to take place
ne quis sciat – 'may no one know' - *sciō, scīre, scīvī, scītum* (4)– to know

...two blind men followed him, crying, and saying, "Son of David, have mercy on us!"
And when he came into the house, the blind men came to him and Jesus saith unto them,
"Do you believe that I am able to do this?" They said unto him, "Yes, Lord."
Then touched he their eyes, saying, "According to your faith be it unto you."
And their eyes were opened, and Jesus demanded of them, saying, "See that no man know it."
But they, when they left, spread the news of this in all that country.

Confiteor – I Confess

***Confiteor Deo omnipoténti, beátæ Mariæ semper Vírgini, beáto Michaéli Archángelo,
beáto Ioánni Baptístæ, sanctis Apóstolis Petro et Paulo, ómnibus Sanctis, et vobis, fratres:
quia peccávi nimis cogitatióne, verbo et ópere mea culpa, mea culpa, mea máxima culpa.***
I confess to almighty God, to blessed Mary ever Virgin, to blessed Michael the Archangel,
to blessed John the Baptist, to the holy Apostles Peter and Paul, to all the Saints, and to you,
brothers, that I have sinned exceedingly in thought, word, and deed, through my fault,
through my fault, through my most grievous fault.

Lesson VII

Posse, Ire, velle/nolle

PISCIS

Remember, we mentioned that the oldest and the most frequently used verbs in any language are usually the most irregular. Examples of such verbs in English are 'to be,' 'can,' 'must.' In Latin we've already encountered a very irregular verb – *esse* = to be. If you know the forms of *esse*, you will easily handle another irregular Latin verb – ***possum, posse, potuī*** = to be able to. *Esse* and *posse* are quite similar. Take a look at their conjugation:

	PRESENT		PAST IMPERFECT		PAST PERFECT	
I	*sum*	*possum*	*eram*	*poteram*	*fui*	*potui*
you	*es*	*potes*	*eras*	*poteras*	*fuisti*	*potuisti*
he/she/it	*est*	*potest*	*erat*	*poterat*	*fuit*	*potuit*
we	*sumus*	*possumus*	*eramus*	*poteramus*	*fuimus*	*potuimus*
you (pl.)	*estis*	*potestis*	*eratis*	*poteratis*	*fuistis*	*potuistis*
they	*sunt*	*possunt*	*erant*	*poterant*	*fuerunt*	*potuerunt*

Omnia possum in eo qui me confortat (Phil. 4:13)
I can do anything through him who gives me strength.

Non potest arbor bona fructus malos facere neque arbor mala fructus bonos facere. (Matt. 7:18)
A good tree cannot bring forth evil fruit, neither can a corrupt tree bring forth good fruit.

Deus, a quo sancta desideria, recta consilia, et justa suiit opera, da servis tuis illam – quam mundus dare non potest – pacem...
O God, from whom [come] holy desires, right advice, and just works, give your servants what the world can not give – peace.

Habere non potest Deum patrem qui ecclesiam non habet matrem. Si potuit evadere quisquis extra arcam Noe fuit, et qui extra ecclesiam fuerit evadit. (Eusebius)
He cannot have God for his Father who has not the Church for his mother. If he could escape who was outside the ark of Noah, then he too will escape who was outside the Church.

Past Perfect: *potuit, fuit*; Present: *potest, habet, evadit*; Future Perfect: *fuerit*

ROSARIUM   ROSAE IN ROSARIO

Two more irregular Latin verbs: *eō, īre, itum* = to go, and *volō, velle, voluī* = to want

The opposite of *velle* is *nolle* = *non* + *velle* – to not want.

The verb *ire* often appears with prefixes, such as *adire* = to approach, *abire* = to leave, and others.

	PRESENT			PAST IMPERFECT			PAST PERFECT		
I	eo	volo	nolo	ibam	volebam	nolebam	ivi	volui	nolui
you	is	vis	non vis	ibas	volebas	nolebas	isti	voluisti	noluisti
he/she/it	it	vult	non vult	ibat	volebat	nolebat	iit	voluit	noluit
we	imus	vimus	nolumus	ibamus	volebamus	nolebamus	iimus	voluimus	noluimus
you (pl.)	itis	vultis	non vultis	ibatis	volebatis	nolebatis	istis	voluistis	noluistis
they	eunt	volunt	nolunt	ibant	volebant	nolebant	ierunt	voluerunt	noluerunt

Beatus homo qui non abiit in consilio impiorum. (Ps.1:1)
Blessed is the man who does not walk in the counsel of the wicked.

Dico autem vobis quia multi prophetae et iusti voluerunt videre quae videtis et non viderunt, et audire quae auditis et non audierunt. (Matt. 13:17)
Verily I say unto you, That many prophets and righteous men have desired to see those things which you see, and have not seen them; and to hear those things which you hear, and have not heard them.

Past Perfect: *voluerunt, viderunt, audierunt*

'Institution of the Eucharist' by Fra Angelico

ACCIPITE ET COMEDITE. HOC EST CORPUS MEUM... HIC EST SANGUIS MEUS NOVI TESTAMENTI, QUI PRO MULTIS EFFUNDITUR IN REMISSIONEM PECCATORUM.

ACCEPIT IESUS PANEM ET BENEDIXIT. ET ACCIPIENS CALICEM, GRATIAS EGIT, ET DEDIT ILLIS.

Subjunctive Mood

> *Crede, ut intelligas.*
> Believe, so that
> you understand.
> (St. Augustine)

Latin verbs have three 'moods.'
The **Indicative mood** states facts: 'I believe.'
The **Imperative mood** expresses commands/requests: 'Believe!'
The *Subjunctive mood* expresses a wish, hope, or condition: 'May you believe.'
Latin prayers are full of Subjunctive mood. Take a look at the first lines of the *Lord's Prayer*:
Páter nóster qui es in cáelis, sanctificétur nomen túum.
sanctificetur – Present Tense Subjunctive, Passive – 'may it be sanctified' –
sanctificō, sanctificāre, sanctificāvī, sanctificātum (1) – to sanctify
Advéniat régnum túum.
adveniat – Present Tense Subjunctive – *adveniō, advenīre, advēnī, adventum* (4) – to arrive
Fíat vóluntas tua sicút in Cáelo et in térra.
fiat – Present Tense Subjunctive – *fīō, fierī, factum* (dep.) – to happen, to take place

Subjunctive mood endings are similar to Present Tense endings.

I	- m
you	- s
he, she, it	- t
we	- mus
you (pl.)	- tis
they	- nt

To form Subjunctive mood, we modify the stem of the verb and add an ending.

1st conjugation: remove *- are* from the infinitive of the verb + *e* + ending
>> *vocare* = to call, *vocem* = may I call
2nd conjugation: remove *- re* from the infinitive of the verb + *a* + ending
>> *habere* = to have, *habeam* = may I have
3rd conjugation: remove *- ere* from the infinitive of the verb + *a* + ending
>> *ducere* = to lead, *ducam* = may I lead
4th conjugation: remove *- re* from the infinitive of the verb + *a* + ending
>> *venire* = to come, *veniam* = may I come

Far less common are **Past Subjunctive** tenses – **Imperfect and Perfect**.
Imperfect Past Subjunctive – add endings from the chart above to the infinitive form of the verb
>> *vocare* + *m* = *vocarem* – 'might I call'
Perfect Past Subjunctive – remove *i* from the 3rd principal part of the verb + *eri* + ending
>> *vocavi* > *vocav* + *eri* + *m* = *vocaverim* – 'might I have called'
Fuit homo missus a Deo, cui nomen erat Joannes. Hic venit in testimonium, ut testimonium perhiberet de lumine, ut omnes crederent per illum. (John 1:18)
There was a man sent by God. His name was John. He came as a witness, to testify to the Light, so that everyone might believe through Him. Subjunctive Imperfect – *perhiberet, crederent*

Another common use of the Subjunctive mood is with the conjunction *ut*.
Ut often appears in the clauses (portions of sentences) that express
– purpose, and can be translated as 'so as,' 'in order to'
– command, and can be translated as 'that'
– possibility, and can be translated as 'that'

arcana – secrets of nature/creation
mysteria – secrets of faith / religion
secreta – secrets made by people, such as tricks, deceit, gossip, etc.

ut + purpose

Credo ut intellegam. (St. Augustine) – I believe so that I may understand.
Subjunctive Present: *intellegam* – *intellegō, intellegere, intellēxī, intellēctum* (3)
Sic luceat lux vestra coram hominibus, ut videant vestra bona opera,
et glorificent Patrem vestrum qui in caelis est.
Let your light so shine before men, that they may see your good works,
and glorify your Father who is in heaven.
Subjunctive Present:
luceat – *lūceō, lūcēre, lūxī* (2) – to shine
videant – *videō, vidēre, vīdī, vīsum* (2) – to see
glorificent – *videō, vidēre, vīdī, vīsum* (2) – to glorify

feria – day of the week
feria quarta – Wednesday
Feria Quarta Cinerum – Ash Wednesday

ut + command

Dixit autem illi diabolus: 'Si Filius Dei es, dic lapidi huic ut panis fiat...' (Luke 4:3)
And the devil said unto him, 'If you are the Son of God, command this stone that it be bread...'
Subjunctive Present: *fiat* – 'may it be' – *fīō, fierī, factum* (dep.) – to happen, to take place

ut + possibility

Domine, non sum dignus ut intres sub tectum meum: sed tantum dic verbo
et sanabitur anima mea.
Lord I am not worthy that You should enter under my roof, but only say the word and
my soul will be healed.
Subjunctive Present: *intres* – 'that you enter' – *intrō, intrāre, intrāvī, intrātum* (1) – to enter
Patres, nolite ad indignationem provocare filios vestros, ut non pusillo animo fiant. (Col. 3:21)
Fathers, don't provoke your children to disdain, that they may not become of feeble mind.
Subjunctive Present: *fiant* – *fīō, fierī, factum* (dep.) – to happen, to take place
Omnia ergo quaecumque vultis ut faciant vobis homines, et vos facite eis. (Matt. 7:12)
Whatsoever things therefore that you wish men should do unto you, do also unto them.
Subjunctive Present: *faciant* – 'that they do' – *faciō, facere, fēcī, factum* (3) – to do

Subjunctive is also commonly used with *cum* = when/while/because:

Cum autem adpropinquaret portae civitatis, et ecce, defunctus efferebatur filius unicus matri suae...

Now when he approached the gates of the city, behold, there was a dead man carried out, the only son of his mother...

Subjunctive Imperfect: *adpropinquaret* = when he was approaching (*adpropinquare*)

Reading Church Latin texts, you will certainly encounter Subjunctive forms of the verb esse:

	Subjunctive Present	Subjunctive Imperfect	Subjunctive Perfect
I	*sim*	*essem*	*fuerim*
you	*sīs*	*esses*	*fueris*
he, she, it	*sit*	*esset*	*fuerit*
we	*sīmus*	*essemus*	*fuerimus*
you (pl.)	*sītis*	*essetis*	*fueritis*
they	*sint*	*essent*	*fuerint*

FLAMMA AETERNAE CARITATIS

Praesta ut sacrificium...tibi sit acceptabile.
Grant that the sacrifice...may be acceptable to You.
Dominus sit in corde meo et in labiis meis...
May the Lord be in my heart and on my lips...
Libera nos, quaesumus, Domine, ab omnibus malis...
ut a peccato simus semper liberi, et ab omni perturbatione securi.
Lord, we beg You to deliver us from every evil...
that we may be always free from sin and safe from every worry.
Ne timeas illam, quae vitae est ultima finis:
Qui mortem metuit amittit gaudia vitae.
(From *Disticha Catonis*)
Do not fear that which is the final end of life:
Whoever fears death misses out on the joys of life.

Present Subjunctive:
timeas – *timeō, timēre, timuī* (2) – to be afraid
mors, mortis, f. (3) – death • *gaudium, gaudiī*, n. (2) – joy

ostendere – to show something that is visible
monstrare – to show = provide information about something

ORATIO MEA

ELEVATIO MANUUM MEARUM

ALTARE

Réquiem Aetérnam – Eternal Rest Prayer

Réquiem ætérnam dona ei (eis) Dómine; et lux perpétua lúceat ei (eis).
Requiéscat (Requiéscant) in pace. Amen.

Eternal rest grant unto him/her (them), O Lord; and let perpetual light shine upon him/her (them).
May he/she (they) rest in peace. Amen.

Subjunctive Present: *lúceat* – 'may shine' – *lūceō, lūcēre, lūxī* (2) – to shine
                requiéscat / requiéscant – 'may he/she/they rest' –
                requiēscō, requiēscere, requiēvī, requiētum (3) – to rest

Dixit autem Maria: 'Ecce ancilla Domini, fiat mihi secundum verbum tuum...' (Luke 1:38)

And Mary said: 'Behold the handmaid of the Lord; be it unto me according to thy word...'

Subjunctive Present: *fiat* – 'may it be' – *fīō, fierī, factum* (dep.) – to happen, to take place

Domine, exaudi orationem meam. Et clamor meus ad te veniat.

Lord, hear my prayer. And let my cry come to You

Subjunctive Present: *veniat* – *veniō, venīre, vēnī, ventum* (4) – to come

servus – a slave servant
ancilla – a female slave servant
minister – a servant or an assistant who is not a slave

Reading

Blessing for a Sick Person

Dóminus Iesus Christus apud te sit, ut te deféndat: intra te sit, ut te consérvet: ante te sit, ut te ducat: post te sit, ut te custódiat: super te sit, ut te benedícat: Qui cum Patre et Spíritu Sancto vivit et regnat in sæcula sæculórum.

Subjunctive Present:

sit – *sum, esse, fuī, futūrum* (irr.) – to be
deféndat – *dēfendō, dēfendere, dēfendī, dēfēnsum* (3) – to defend
consérvet – *cōnservō, cōnservāre, cōnservāvī, cōnservātum* (1) – to save, keep
ducat – *dūcō, dūcere, dūxī, ductum* (3) – to lead
custódiat – *custōdiō, custōdīre, custōdīvī, custōdītum* (4) – to guard
benedícat – *benedīcō, benedīcere, benedīxī, benedictum* (3) – to bless

Present Tense:

vivit – *vīvō, vīvere, vīxī, vīctum* (3) – to live
regnat – *rēgnō, rēgnāre, rēgnāvī, rēgnātum* (1) – to reign

mittere – to send
dimittere – to let go

festum – feast
Festum Magorum or *Festum Regum*
the Epiphany

May the Lord Jesus Christ be with you that He may defend you; within you that He may sustain you; before you that He may lead you; behind you that He may protect you; above you that He may bless you; He Who lives and reigns with the Father and the Holy Spirit for ever and ever. Amen.

...*accessit ad eum centurio rogans eum et dicens:* "*Domine, puer meus iacet in domo paralyticus et male torquetur.*" *Et ait illi Iesus:* "*Ego veniam et curabo eum.*" *Et respondens centurio ait:* "*Domine, non sum dignus ut intres sub tectum meum, sed tantum dic verbo et sanabitur puer meus. Nam et ego homo sum sub potestate, habens sub me milites, et dico huic 'vade' – et vadit, et alio 'veni' – et venit, et servo meo 'fac hoc' – et facit.*" *Audiens autem, Iesus miratus est et sequentibus se dixit:* "*Amen dico vobis, non inveni tantam fidem in Israhel!*"......*Et dixit Iesus centurioni:* "*Vade, et sicut credidisti fiat tibi.*" *Et sanatus est puer in hora illa.*

Present Participles: rogans, dicens, respondens, habens, audiens
rogans << *rogō, rogāre, rogāvī, rogātum* (1) – to ask
Past Participle: miratus – 'amazed' – *mīror, mīrārī, mīrātum* (dep.) – to wonder
Imperative Mood: dic, vade, veni, fac • vade << *vādō, vādere* (3) – go, walk
Present Tense:
iacet – *iaceō, iacēre, iacuī, iacitūrum* (2) – to lie
torquetur – Present, passive – *torqueō, torquēre, torsī, tortum* (2) – to twist, to torture
Past Perfect:
accessit – *accēdō, accēdere, accessī, accessum* (3) – approach
inveni – *inveniō, invenīre, invēnī, inventum* (4) – to find
credidisti – *crēdō, crēdere, crēdidī, crēditum* (3) – to believe

genetrix, genetricis, f. (3)
mother, ancestor
Genetrix – the Mother of God

Future:
veniam, curabo – *ūrō, cūrāre, cūrāvī, cūrātum* (1) – to take care, to cure
sanabitur – Future, passive – *sānō, sānāre, sānāvī, sānātum* (1) – to cure
Subjunctive Present: intres – *intrō, intrāre, intrāvī, intrātum* (1) – to enter
fiat – *fīō, fierī, factum* (dep.) – to happen, to take place

...there came unto him a centurion, beseeching him, and saying, "Lord, my servant lies at home sick of the palsy, grievously tormented." And Jesus said unto him, "I will come and heal him." The centurion answered and said, "Lord, I am not worthy that you should come under my roof: but speak the word only, and my servant shall be healed. For I, too, am a man under authority, having soldiers under me. And I say to this man, Go, and he goes; and to another, Come, and he comes; and to my servant, Do this, and he does it." When Jesus heard it, he marvelled, and said to them that followed him, "Verily I say unto you, I have not found such great faith in Israel."...And Jesus said unto the centurion, "Go your way; and as you have believed, so be it done unto you." And his servant was healed that same hour.

flamma, flammae, f. (1) – flame • *flāmen, flāminis,* f. (3) – wind, breath
Flamen Supernum – the Divine Breath, the Holy Ghost

LESSON VIII — Future Tense

Just like Past tenses, Latin future tenses distinguish between completed and incomplete or repeated actions.

In the **Simple Future**, or **Future Imperfect** tense, Latin verbs have the same endings as in the Present tense, but the stem of the verb changes a bit, ending in

- *b*, - *bu*, or - *bi* in the 1st and 2nd Conjugation verbs
- *e* in the 3rd and 4th Conjugation verbs, except the 'I' form that has - *a* instead of - *e* at the end of its stem with the ending - *m* instead of - *o*

	1st and 2nd Conjugation		3rd and 4th Conjugation	
I	- bo	habebo	- am	veniam
you	- bis	habebis	- es	venies
he,she,it	- bit	habebit	- et	veniet
we	- bimus	habebimus	- emus	veniemus
you (pl.)	- bitis	habebitis	- etis	venietis
they	- bunt	habebunt	- ent	venient

Dominus providebit – The Lord will provide
providebit – *prōvideō, prōvidēre, prōvīdī, prōvīsum* (2) – to provide

abscondere – to hide
quaerere – to seek

Petite et accipiétis; quaérite et inveniétis; pulsate et aperiétur vobis...
Ask and you shall receive, seek and you shall find, knock and it shall be opened unto you...
accipietis – *accipiō, accipere, accēpī, acceptum* (3) – to receive
invenietis – *inveniō, invenīre, invēnī, inventum* (4) – to find

Si enim diligatis eos qui vos diligunt quam mercedem habebitis? (Matt. 5:46)
For if you love them which love you, what reward have you?

invenire – to find
claudere – to close
aperire – to open

habebitis – *habeō, habēre, habuī, habitum* (2) – to have

Non relinquam vos orphanos: veniam ad vos. (John 14:18)
I will not leave you orphans: I will come to you.
relinquam – *relinquō, relinquere, relīquī, relictum* (3) – to leave behind, to abandon
veniam – *veniō, venīre, vēnī, ventum* (4) – to come

Et ait [diabolus] ei: "Tibi dabo potestatem hanc universam et gloriam illorum." (Luke 4:6)
And the devil said unto him, All this power will I will give you, and the glory of these...
dabo – *dō, dare, dedī, datum* (irr.) – to give

Et videbit omnis caro salutare Dei. (Luke 3:6) – And all flesh shall see the salvation of God.
videbit – *video, vidēre, vīdī, vīsum* (2) – to see

Et cognoscetis veritatem et veritas liberabit vos. (John 8:32)
And you will know the truth, and the truth shall set you free.
cognoscetis – cōgnōscō, cōgnōscere, cōgnōvī, cōgnitum (3) – to recognize
liberabit – līberō, līberāre, līberāvī, līberātum (1) – to liberate
Venite ad me omnes qui laboratis et onerati estis et ego reficiam vos (Matthew 11:28)
Come to me, all you who are weary and burdened, and I will give you rest.
reficiam – reficiō, reficere, refēcī, refectum (3) – to restore, to repair

And here are our irregular verbs – *esse* and *ire* – in the simple Future Tense:

	esse	ire
I	ero	ibo
you	eris	ibis
he, she, it	erit	ibit
we	erimus	ibimus
you (pl.)	eritis	ibitis
they	erunt	ibunt

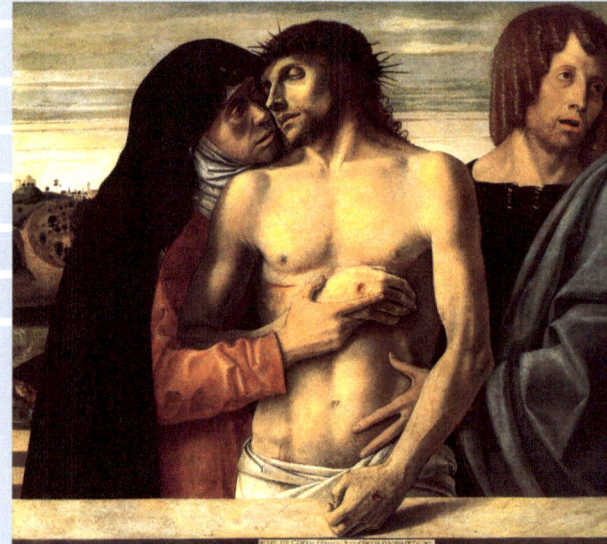

'Dead Christ' by Giovanni Bellini

...cuius regni non erit finis...
...whose kingdom will have no end... *regnum*, n. (2)
Introibo ad altare Dei...
I will enter the altar of God... *altare, altaris*, n. (3)

If your head is spinning from the complexity of the so-called Simple Future tense, brace yourself for the nearly impossible **Future Perfect tense**! ...Just kidding! It's one of the easiest verbal forms because the verbs of all conjugations use the same endings for the Future Perfect tense. The Future Perfect tense is used to describe an action that will be completed in the future. For example, "By that time I will have finished my work." To form the Future Perfect tense just remove the final *i* from the 3rd principal part of the verb (for example, *amavi* >> *amav*), and add the personal endings from the chart below.

I	- ero	we	- erimus
you	- eris	you (pl.)	- eritis
he, she, it	- erit	they	- erint

Omnis enim quicumque invocaverit nomen Domini salvus erit. (Romans 10:13)
For whosoever shall call upon the name of the Lord shall be saved.
invocaverit – will have invoked – Future Perfect –
invocō, invocāre, invocāvī, invocātum (1) – to call upon, to invoke
erit – will be – Simple Future – *sum, esse, fuī, futūrum* (irr.)

from *Psalmus 129*
De profundis clamavi ad te, Domine: Domine, exaudi vocem meam.
Fiant aures tuae intendentes, in vocem deprecationis meae.
Si iniquitates observaveris, Domine: Domine, quis sustinēbit?
Out of the depths I have cried to You, O Lord: Lord, hear my voice.
Let Your ears be attentive to the voice of my supplication.
If You, Lord, should notice iniquities, O Lord, who shall stand?

Simple/Imperfect Future: *sustinēbit* – *sustineō, sustinēre, sustinuī, sustentum* (2) – to sustain
Future Perfect tense:
observaveris – you will notice – *observō, observāre, observāvī, observātum* (1) – to watch
Subjunctive:
fiant – may they be – *fīō, fierī, factum* (dep.) – to happen, to take place

revereri –
to feel reverence
venerare – to show reverence for the sacred
observare – to respect, to observe a custom
adorare – to worship
admirare – to express admiration/enthusiasm

'Entry in Jerusalem' by Fra Angelico

BENEDICTUS REX QUI VENIT IN NOMINE DOMINI!

IESUS ASCENDIT IN HIEROSOLYMA. VIDENS HIEROSOLYMA, FLEVIT SUPER ILLAM.

DISCIPULI

SI HII TACUERINT LAPIDES CLAMABUNT.

PAX IN CAELO! GLORIA IN EXCELSIS!

VESTIMENTA IN VIA

OSANNA FILIO DAVID BENEDICTVS QVI VENIT IN NOMINE DOMINI. MACTEI. XXI.

Irregular verbs *esse*, *posse* and *ire* – Future Perfect tense:

	esse	posse	ire
I	fuerō	potuerō	ierō
you	fueris	potueris	ieris
he, she, it	fuerit	potuerit	ierit
we	fuerimus	potuerimus	ierimus
you (pl.)	fueritis	potueritis	ieritis
they	fuerint	potuerint	ierint

fidere – to feel trust toward a person/an idea
credere – to place one's belief intentionally and rationally in a person/idea

Respondit Iesus et dixit ei: 'Amen, amen dico tibi, nisi quis natus fuerit denuo non potest videre regnum Dei.' (John 3:3)

Jesus replied, 'Very truly I tell you, no one can see the kingdom of God without being born again.'

natus fuerit – will be born – Future Perfect

Passive Voice

The passive voice occurs in all tenses. In the Imperfect tenses – Present, Imperfect Past and Simple/Imperfect Future – passive endings are simply added to the stem required by this or that tense. The easiest way to grasp this is to notice the stem changes and the endings across the 4 conjugations in the following examples:

vocō, vocāre, vocāvī, vocātum (1) – to call
habeō, habēre, habuī, habitum (2) – to have
dūcō, dūcere, dūxī, ductum (3) – to lead
audiō, audīre, audīvī, audītum (4) – to hear

delictum – breaking of rules due to carelessness
peccatum – transgression of the laws of God or reason
malefactum – misdeed, misstep
maleficium – evil deed caused by evil intention
impietas – offence against piety

Present Tense – Passive Voice

Conjugation	1	2	3	4
	being called	being had	being led	being heard
I	vocor	habeor	dūcor	audior
you	vocāris	habēris	dūceris	audīris
he, she, it	vocātur	habētur	dūcitur	audītur
we	vocāmur	habēmur	dūcimur	audīmur
you (pl.)	vocāminī	habēminī	dūciminī	audīminī
they	vocantur	habentur	dūcuntur	audiuntur

Imperfect Past tense – Passive Voice

Conjugation	1	2	3	4
	being called	being had	being led	being heard
I	*vocābar*	*habēbar*	*dūcēbar*	*audiēbar*
you	*vocābāris*	*habēbāris*	*dūcēbāris*	*audiēbāris*
he, she, it	*vocābātur*	*habēbātur*	*dūcēbātur*	*audiēbātur*
we	*vocābāmur*	*habēbāmur*	*dūcēbāmur*	*audiēbāmur*
you (pl.)	*vocābāminī*	*habēbāminī*	*dūcēbāminī*	*audiēbāminī*
they	*vocābantur*	*habēbantur*	*dūcēbantur*	*audiēbantur*

Simple Future tense – Passive Voice

Conjugation	1	2	3	4
	being called	being had	being led	being heard
I	*vocābor*	*habēbor*	*dūcar*	*audiar*
you	*vocāberis*	*habēberis*	*dūcēris*	*audiēris*
he, she, it	*vocābitur*	*habēbitur*	*dūcētur*	*audiētur*
we	*vocābimur*	*habēbimur*	*dūcēmur*	*audiēmur*
you (pl.)	*vocābiminī*	*habēbiminī*	*dūcēminī*	*audiēminī*
they	*vocābuntur*	*habēbuntur*	*dūcentur*	*audientur*

At illi instabant vocibus magnis postulantes ut crucifigeretur. (Luke 23:23)
But they were urgent with loud voices demanding that he should be crucified.
crucifigeretur – Imperfect Subjunctive, passive –
crucīfīgō, crucīfīgere, crucīfīxī, crucīfīxum (3) – to crucify
Quaerite autem primum regnum et iustitiam eius et omnia haec adicientur vobis. (Matt. 6:33)
But seek first the kingdom of God, and his righteousness; and all these things shall
be added unto you. – *adicientur* – Future Perfect – *adiciō, adicere, adiēcī, adiectum* (3) – to add
Vincere cum possis, interdum cede sodali;
Obsequio quoniam dulces retinentur amici. (From *Disticha Catonis*)
When you can win, from time to time give in to a friend;
Sometimes good friends are kept by giving in.
retinentur – 'are kept' – from *retineō, retinēre, retinuī, retentum* (2) – to keep

amare = to love; *diligere* – to feel esteem toward = to love
caritas = selfless love, affection; *pietas* = love for God, holy things, one's family, or country

Passive voice in the Perfect tenses is easy.

Past Participle + forms of *esse* >>

vocatus sum = I was called

vocatus ero = I will have been called...

agere – to do, to act

facere – to make, to create

Nolite iudicare et non iudicabimini, nolite condemnare et non condemnabimini, dimittite et dimittemini, date et dabitur vobis... (Luke 37-38)

Judge not, and you shall not be judged: Condemn not, and you shall not be condemned: Forgive, and you shall be forgiven: Give, and it shall be given unto you...

Passive Future:

iudicabimini – *iūdicō, iūdicāre, iūdicāvī, iūdicātum* (1) – to judge, to sentence

condemnabimini – *condemnō, condemnāre, condemnāvī, condemnātum* (1) – to condemn

dimittemini – *dīmittō, dīmittere, dīmīsī, dīmissum* (3) – to let go

Beati qui nunc fletis, quia ridebitis. Beati eritis cum vos oderint homines et cum separaverint vos et exprobraverint et eiecerint nomen vestrum tamquam malum propter Filium hominis. (Luke 6:21-22)

Blessed are you that weep now: for you shall laugh.

Blessed are you, when men shall hate you, and when they shall separate you from their company, and shall reproach you, and cast out your name as evil, for the Son of man's sake.

Passive Voice Future: *beati eritis*

Future Imperfect: *ridebitis – rīdeō, rīdēre, rīsī, rīsum* (2) – to laugh

Future Perfect, 'they' forms:

oderint – *ōdī, ōdisse, ōdī, ōsum* (4) – to hate

separaverint – *sēparō, sēparāre, sēparāvī, sēparātum* (1) – to divide, separate

exprobraverint – *exprobrō, exprobrāre, exprobrāvī, exprobrātum* (1) – to reproach

eiecerint – *iaciō, iacere, iēcī, iactum* (3) – to throw, to cast out

Verbs also have **passive infinitive** forms. In the passage below

abscondi = 'to be hidden' is a passive infinitive of the verb

abscondō, abscondere, abscondī, absconditum (3) – to hide

Vos estis lux mundi. Non potest civitas abscondi supra montem posita. (Matt. 5:14)

You are the light of the world. A city that is set on a hill cannot be hidden.

lacrimare – to shed tears silently • *flere* – to shed tears and express grief vocally, to weep

plorare – to express grief vocally, to wail, to cry • *lamentare* – to wail without stopping

Deponent Verbs

Some Latin verbs are passive in form, but have active meanings. For example, *confiteor* = I confess, is an active verb, but with the forms of a passive verb. Such verbs are called **deponent verbs**. They include:

loquor, loquī, locūtum (dep.) – to speak
patior, patī, passum (dep.) – to suffer
morior, morī, mortuum (dep.) – to die
nāscor, nāscī, nātum (dep.) – to be born
mīror, mīrārī, mīrātum (dep.) – to wonder, to marvel
revertor, revertī, reversum (dep.) – to turn back, to return
calumnior, calumniārī, calumniātum (dep.) – to falsely accuse

> *dicere* – to say
> *loqui* – to talk
> *aio (ait)* – to state
> *inquere (inquit)* – to state, to affirm
> *affirmare* – to state emphatically
> *fari* – to speak (as opposed to making animal sounds)

Remember this passage from the *Apostles' Creed* using a few deponent verbs?
...qui conceptus est de Spiritu Sancto, natus ex Maria Virgine, passus sub Pontio Pilato, crucifixus, mortuus, et sepultus...

More examples using deponent verbs:
Memento mori = Remember about dying/death
Confitemini Domino quoniam bonus...
Praise the Lord, for He is good...
confitemini << *cōnfiteor, cōnfitērī, cōnfessum* (dep.)
Et accedens Iesus locutus est, eis dicens: 'Data est mihi omnis potestas in caelo et in terra.' (Matthew 28:18)
And Jesus came and spoke unto them, saying, 'All power is given unto me in heaven and on earth.'

> *mori* – to die (naturally)
> *perire* – to perish

Present participles:
accedens – *accēdō, accēdere, accessī, accessum* (3) – to approach
dicens – *dīcō, dīcere, dīxī, dictum* (3) – to say
Past participle with Active Voice meaning: *locutus est* – *loquor, loquī, locūtum* – to speak
Et reversi sunt pastores glorificantes et laudantes Deum. (Luke 2:20)
And the shepherds returned, glorifying and praising God.
Present participles: *glorificantes et laudantes*
glorificō, glorificāre, glorificāvī, glorificātum (1) – to glorify
laudō, laudāre, laudāvī, laudātum (1) – to praise
Past participle with Active Voice meaning: *reversi sunt*

> *dolor* – feeling of grief
> *tristitia* – expression of sadness in gestures and and behavior

...*natus est vobis hodie salvator qui est Christus Dominus*...(Luke 2:11)

...unto you is born this day a Saviour, which is Christ the Lord...

Past participle with Active Voice meaning: *natus est*

Et omnes qui audierunt mirati sunt... (Luke 2:18)

And all they that heard it wondered...

Past participle with Active Voice meaning: *mirati sunt*

Iesus autem plenus Spiritu Sancto regressus est ab Iordane et agebatur in Spiritu in desertum diebus quadraginta et temptabatur a diabolo...(Luke 4:1)

And Jesus being full of the Holy Spirit returned from Jordan, and was led by the Spirit into the wilderness being forty days tempted of the devil...

Past participle with Active Voice meaning:

regressus est – [he] returned – Past Perfect – *regredior, regredī, regressum* (dep.) – to return

Passive Voice verbs:

agebatur – [he] was led – Imperfect, Passive – *agō, agere, ēgī, āctum* (3) – to act, to drive

temptabatur – [he] was tempted – Imperfect, Passive –

temptō, temptāre, temptāvī, temptātum (1) – to tempt, to test

salvus – safe, saved = not perishing
integer – safe = untouched

'The Garden of Gethsemane' by Fra Angelico

ferre – to carry a burden
tolerare – to carry a burden willingly
tollere – to lift, to take away
sustinere – to support

SI POSSIBILE EST TRANSEAT A ME CALIX ISTE.

TRISTIS EST ANIMA MEA USQUE AD MORTEM. SUSTINETE HIC ET VIGILATE MECUM.

IESUS ORAT. DISCIPULI DORMIUNT.

SPIRITUS PROMPTUS EST, CARO AUTEM INFIRMA!

ARBOR

FLORES

ave – 'hi' and 'bye,' rejoice
salve – 'hi,' 'greetings'
vale – 'bye'

READING

Beati pauperes spiritu quoniam ipsorum est regnum caelorum.
Blessed are the poor in spirit: for theirs is the kingdom of heaven.

Beati mites quoniam ipsi possidebunt terram.
Blessed are the meek: for they shall inherit the earth.

possidebunt – Simple Future – *possīdō, possīdere, possēdī, possessum* (3) – to own

Beati qui lugent quoniam ipsi consolabuntur.
Blessed are they that mourn: for they shall be comforted.

lugent – Present tense – *lūgeō, lūgēre, lūxī, lūctum* (2) – to mourn
consolabuntur – Simple Future – *cōnsōlor, cōnsōlārī, cōnsōlātum* (dep.) – to console

Beati qui esuriunt et sitiunt iustitiam quoniam ipsi saturabuntur.
Blessed are they which do hunger and thirst after righteousness: for they shall be filled.

esuriunt – Present tense – *ēsuriō, ēsurīre, ēsurīvī, ēsuritūrum* (4) – to be hungry
sitiunt – Present tense – *sitiō, sitīre, sitīvī, sitītum* (4) – to be thirsty
saturabuntur – Simple Future, passive – *saturō, saturāre, saturāvī, saturātum* (1) – to satisfy

Beati misericordes quia ipsi misericordiam consequentur.
Blessed are the merciful: for they shall obtain mercy.

consequentur – Simple Future - *cōnsequor, cōnsequī, cōnsecūtum* (dep.) – to follow

Beati mundo corde quoniam ipsi Deum videbunt.
Blessed are the pure in heart: for they shall see God.

videbunt – Simple Future – *videō, vidēre, vīdī, vīsum* (2) – to see

Beati pacifici quoniam filii Dei vocabuntur.
Blessed are the peacemakers: for they shall be called the children of God.

vocabuntur – Simple Future, passive – *vocō, vocāre, vocāvī, vocātum* (1) – to call

Beati qui persecutionem patiuntur propter iustitiam quoniam ipsorum est regnum caelorum.
Blessed are they which are persecuted for righteousness' sake: for theirs is the kingdom of heaven.

patiuntur – Present tense – *patior, patī, passum* (dep.) – to suffer

Beati estis cum maledixerint vobis et persecuti vos fuerint et dixerint omne malum adversum vos mentientes propter me. Blessed are you, when men shall revile you, and persecute you, and shall say all manner of evil against you falsely, for my sake.

maledixerint – Future Perfect – *maledīcō, maledīcere, maledīxī, maledictum* (3) – to slander
persecuti – Past participle – *persequor, persequī, persecūtum* (dep.) – to persecute
fuerint – Future Perfect – *sum, esse, fuī, futūrum* (irr.) – to be
dixerint – Future Perfect – *dīcō, dīcere, dīxī, dictum* (3) – to say

---

videre – to see
spectare – to look
conspicere – to gaze at

bonus – good
probus – upright, just
honestus – honorable

habere – to have, to own
tenere – to hold
possidere – to possess, to own

Et accedentes discipuli dixerunt ei: 'Quare in parabolis loqueris eis?'
Qui respondens ait illis: 'Quia vobis datum est nosse mysteria regni caelorum, illis autem non est datum. Qui enim habet dabitur ei et abundabit. Qui autem non habet et quod habet auferetur ab eo. Ideo in parabolis loquor eis, quia videntes non vident et audientes non audiunt neque intellegunt...' (Matt. 13:10-13)

The disciples came to him and asked, "Why do you speak to the people in parables?" He replied, "Because the knowledge of the secrets of the kingdom of heaven has been given to you, but not to them. Whoever has will be given more, and they will have an abundance. Whoever does not have, even what they have will be taken from them. This is why I speak to them in parables: Though seeing, they do not see; though hearing, they do not hear or understand..."

accedentes – Present Participle – *accēdō, accēdere, accessī, accessum* (3) – to approach

dixerunt – Past Perfect – *dīcō, dīcere, dīxī, dictum* (3) – to speak

loqueris – Present tense – *loquor, loquī, locūtum* (dep.) – to talk

respondens – Present Participle – *respondeō, respondēre, respondī, respōnsum* (2) – to answer

ait – Past Perfect – *āiō, āiere* (3.) – to confirm, to say 'yes'

datum est – Past Participle – *dō, dare, dedī, datum* (irr.) – to give

dabitur – Simple Future, passive – *dare* = to give

abundabit – Simple Future – *abundō, abundāre, abundāvī, abundātum* (1) – to abound

auferetur – Simple Future, passive – *auferō, auferre, abstulī, ablātum* (irr.) – to take away

videntes, audientes – Present Participles

Dicit illis: 'Vos autem quem me esse dicitis?' Respondens Simon Petrus dixit, 'Tu es Christus, Filius Dei vivi.' Respondens autem Iesus dixit ei, 'Beatus es, Simon Bar Iona, quia caro et sanguis non revelavit tibi, sed Pater meus, qui in caelis est. Et ego dico tibi quia tu es Petrus et super hanc petram aedificabo ecclesiam meam, et portae inferi non praevalebunt adversum eam.'

revelavit – Past Perfect

edificabo – Simple Future

He said unto them, 'But whom say you that I am?'
And Simon Peter answered and said, 'You are the Christ, the Son of the living God.' And Jesus answered and said unto him, 'Blessed you are, Simon Bar–jona: for flesh and blood have not revealed it unto you, but my Father which is in heaven. And I say also to you, that you are Peter, and upon this rock I will build my church; and the gates of hell shall not prevail against it.'

Genitive ▬▬ Ablative ▬▬ Accusative ▬▬ Dative ▬▬

LESSON IX

Comparative Degrees of Adjectives and Adverbs

The **comparative degree** forms of most Latin adjectives have the ending **-ior** for the masculine and feminine genders >>
longus, longa – longior = longer • **altus, alta – altior** = higher
-ius for the neuter gender >> **longum – longius** = longer, **altum – altius** = higher
These adjectives decline like 3rd Declension nouns.
Beatius est magis dare quam accipere. (Acts 20:35)
It is more blessed to give than to receive.
The **superlative degree** forms of most Latin adjectives have the ending **-issimus** for the masculine gender >>
longus – longissimus = the longest • **altus – altissimus** = the highest
-issima for the feminine gender >> **longa – longissima** • **alta – altissima**
-issimum for the neuter gender >> **longum – longissimum** • **altum – altissimum**

'Healing of the blind' by Andrei Riabushkin

- QUID TIBI VIS FACIAM?
- FIDES TUA TE SALVUM FECIT!
- DOMINE, UT VIDEAM...
- CAECUS
- CAECI VISUM DAT

'Kiss of Judas' by Giotto

- IUDAS, UNUS DE DUODECIM, VENIT.
- IUDAS OSCULATUS EST EUM.
- TURBA MULTA CUM GLADIIS
- MONS
- ARBOR
- GLADIUS IN MANU
- CONVERTE GLADIUM TUUM IN LOCUM SUUM! OMNES QUI ACCEPERINT GLADIUM, GLADIO PERIBUNT!
- DISCIPULI FUGERUNT.

lux beatissima – the most blessed light
in conspéctu Altíssimi – in the sight of the Most High
Tu solus Altissimus, Jesu Christe. – You alone are most high, Jesus Christ.
from *Laudes Divinae*:
Benedictum Cor Eius sacratissimum. – Blessed be His Most Sacred Heart.
Benedictus Sanguis Eius pretiosissimus. – Blessed be His Most Precious Blood.
Maria sanctissima – Mary most Holy
Benedictus Iésus in Sanctissimo Altaris Saccraménto.
Blessed be Jesus in the Most Holy Sacrament of the Altar.
Benedictus sanctus Ioseph, eius castissimus Sponsus.
Blessed be St. Joseph, her most chaste spouse.

felix – happy
faustus – fortunate
beatus – blessed

sacer – sacred – belonging to God
sanctus – holy (*under the divine protection* in classical Latin)

sacratus – consecrated (Past Participle) • *pretiosus* – precious • *sanctus* – holy • *castus* – pure
Príncepes gloriosíssime coeléstis milítiae, sancte Míchael Archángele, defénde nos in proélio.
O Glorious Prince of the heavenly host, St. Michael the Archangel, defend us in the battle.
gloriosíssime is the Vocative case of *gloriosíssimus*
En ego, o bone et dulcissime Iesu, ante conspectum tuum genibus me provolvo.
Behold, o kind and most sweet Jesus, I cast myself upon my knees in your sight.
dulcis – sweet

Adjectives whose stems end in a vowel use the words
magis = more, and *maxime* = most to form their comparison degrees.
pius, magis pius, maxime pius – more / most godly
O piissima Virgo Maria – O most gracious Virgin Mary

As always the most frequently used adjectives have
the most irregular comparative and superlative degrees.
bonus, melior, optimus – good, better, best
malus, peior, pessimus – bad, worse, worst
magnus, maior, maximus – great, greater, greatest
parvus, minor, minimus – small, smaller, smallest
multus, plus, plurimus – much, more, most

mea máxima culpa – my most grievous fault
Ad Maiorem Dei Gloriam –
for the greater glory of God (motto of the Jesuit order)

'What is truth?' by Nikolai Ge

MEUM REGNUM NON EST HINC. QUI EST EX VERITATE AUDIT MEAM VOCEM.

QUID EST VERITAS?

NULLAM INVENIO IN EO CAUSAM.

Et in hac Trinitate nihil prius aut posterius, nihil maius aut minus: Sed totae tres personae coaéternae sibi sunt et coaéquales. – And in this Trinity none is before or after another; none is greater or less than another. But the whole three Persons are coeternal, and coequal.
prius, posterius, maius, minus – are neuter singular comparative degrees of
prior – preceding, *posterus* – following, *magnus* – great, *parvus* – small

In classical Latin most adverbs end in **- e** >> *facile* – easily
Exiguum munus cum dat tibi pauper amicus,
Accipito placide, plene laudare memento. (from *Disticha Catonis*)
When your poor friend gives you a small gift,
Accept it happily and remember to praise fully.

altare maius – a high altar
altare minus – a side altar

However in the *Vulgata* we find a lot of adverbs ending in **- ter**.
This reflects St. Jerome's choice of the popular, rather than scholarly, style of Latin.

Comparative degrees of adverbs end in **- ius** >> *facilius* – more easily
Superlative degrees of adverbs end in **- issime, - errime, - illime** >> *facillime* – most easily
Irregular adverbs include
multum – much, *paulum* – a little, *magis* – more, *minus* – less,
plus – more, *minime* – least, *plurimum* – most
Deus, qui humanae substantiae dignitatem mirabiliter condidisti et mirabilius reformasti...
O God, who wonderfully created human nature and even more wonderfully restored it...

Latin word *quam* = than often appears in the context of comparison.
...dilexisti malum magis quam bonum, mendacium magis quam loqui iustitiam... (*Psalmus* 52)
... you love evil more than good, lies more than to speak the truth...

Special Uses of the Ablative Case

Phrases like 'greater than,' 'smaller than' are often rendered in Latin without 'than,' by combining a comparative/superlative degree of an adjective with the Ablative case – **Ablative of Comparison**.
minor Patre = less than the Father
Perféctus Deus, perfectus homo: ex anima rationali et humana carné subsistens.
Aéqualis Patri secundum divinitatem: minor Patre secundum humanitatem.
Perfect God; and perfect Man, of a thinking soul and human flesh subsisting.
Equal to the Father, in terms of divinity; and less than the Father in terms of being human.

Along with the Ablative of Comparison, there are many other special uses of the Ablative Case. One of them is the **Ablative Instrumental.**

In English we use prepositions to express the idea of an instrument or method, or 'something done by someone': I write with a pen. Nature is created by God.

In these 'instrumental' contexts Latin does not use any prepositions. It uses only the Ablative case of the word describing the instrument or the person performing the action.

Peccávi nimis cogitatióne, verbo et ópere; mea culpa, mea culpa, mea máxima culpa.
I have sinned exceedingly in/by thought, word, and deed, through/by my fault, through my fault, through my most grievous fault.

verbo, opere, culpa – are the instances of the Ablative Instrumental
verbum, verbī, n (2) – word • *opus, operis,* n (3) – action • *culpa, culpae,* f (1) – fault

Angele Dei, qui custos es mei, me tibi commissum pietate superna; (hodie, hac nocte) illumina, custodi, rege et guberna. Amen. – Angel of God, my guardian dear, to whom his love commits me here; ever this (day, night) be at my side, to light and guard, to rule and guide. Amen.

pietate superna – by/through heavenly piety/love – Ablative instrumental – *pietas superna*
pietās, pietātis, f. (3) – piety, loyalty
supernus – adjective – heavenly (Medieval latin)
commissum = Past Participle of *committō, committere, commīsī, commissum* (3) – to commit

Another use of Ablative Instrumental indicates sensation, emotion, or any condition of the human body or mind:

lux – streaming light
lux solis (sun)
lumen – a luminous body
lumen lucernae (lamp)

Beati pauperes spiritu. (Matt. 5:3) – Blessed are the poor in spirit.
spiritu – Ablative case of *spīritus, spīritūs,* m. (4)
Beati mundo corde. (Matt. 5:8) – Blessed are the pure in/by heart.
mundus – pure, *cor, cordis,* n. (3) – heart

Domine Iesu Christe, qui dixisti: Petite et accipietis; quaerite et invenietis; pulsate et aperietur vobis; quaesumus, da nobis petentibus divinissimi tui amoris affectum, ut te toto corde, ore et opere diligamus et a tua numquam laude cessemus.
O Lord Jesus Christ, who have said: Ask and you shall receive, seek and you shall find, knock and it shall be opened unto you; mercifully attend to our supplications, and grant us the gift of Your divine charity, that we may ever love You with our whole heart and with all our words and deeds, and may never cease praising You.

Ablative Instrumental:
toto corde, ore et opere • *cor, cordis,* n (3) - heart • *ōs, ōris,* n (3) - mouth
Past Perfect Tense: *dixisti* – *dīcō, dīcere, dīxī, dictum* (3) – to say

Simple Future Tense: *accipietis, invenietis*
accipiō, accipere, accēpī, acceptum (3) – to receive
inveniō, invenīre, invēnī, inventum (4) – to find

Passive Voice Future: *aperietur* – *aperiō, aperīre, aperuī, apertum* (4) – to open
nobis petentibus – from *petens,* **Present participle** of *petō, petere, petīvī, petītum* (3) – to ask
divinissimi tui amoris – *amor, amōris,* m. (3) – love

Subjunctive Present: *diligamus, cessemus*
dīligō, dīligere, dīlēxī, dīlēctum (3) – to love
cessō, cessāre, cessāvī, cessātum (1) – to stop, to delay

amicus – a friend
sodalis – a close friend
socius – a partner

summus – the uppermost
supremus – the greatest

O Mater pietatis et misericordiae, beatissima Virgo Maria, ego miser et indignus peccator ad te confugio toto corde et affectu; et precor pietatem tuam...
O Mother of mercy and of love, most blessed Virgin Mary, I, a poor and unworthy sinner, run to you with all my heart and all my affection, and implore thy loving-kindness.

Ablative Instrumental:
toto corde et affectu – *cor, cordis,* n (3), *affectus, affectūs,* m. (4) – mood, affection
pietās, pietātis, f. (3) – piety, loyalty, *misericordia, misericordiae,* f. (1) – compassion

Deponent verb:
precor, precārī, precātum (dep.) – to beg, to pray

petere – to ask for something
rogare – to ask about something

Yet another special use of the Ablative Case is the so-called

Ablative Absolute – noun/pronoun + a participle in the Ablative case.
Ablative Absolute can indicate time or circumstances of an action.
It's similar to the English constructions: 'a news having been heard,' 'a book being read,' etc.
sede vacante – 'the seat being vacant' (a period following the death or resignation of a bishop)
Ablative Case of
sēdēs, sēdis, f. (3) – seat
vacans – present participle formed from *vacō, vacāre, vacāvī, vacātum* (1) – to be empty

In *Vulgata* St. Jerome often uses Ablative Absolute in place of participles.
Et ejecto daemone, locutus est mutus. (Matt.9:33)
And when the devil was was driven out, the dumb man spoke.
ejecto daemone – from *daemon ejectus* – *daemon, daemōnis,* m. (3)

purus – pure, unpolluted
mundus – clean, not dirty

Genitive   Ablative   Accusative   Dative

'Crucifixion' by Fra Angelico

Et ascendente eo in navicula secuti sunt eum discipuli eius. (Matt. 8:23)

And when he entered a ship, his disciples followed him.

Ablative Absolute: 'he, having entered' = *ascendente eo*

Et ecce tota civitas exiit obviam Iesu, et viso eo, rogabant ut transiret a finibus eorum. (Matt. 8:34) – And, behold, the whole city came out to meet Jesus: and when they saw him, they besought him that he would depart out of their coasts.

Ablative Absolute: 'having seen him' = *viso eo* • *obviam* = against, coming toward

Paulo autem volente intrare in populum non permiserunt discipuli. (Acts 19:30)

And when Paul wanted to join the crowd, the disciples did not let him.

Ablative Absolute: 'Paul wanting to' = *Paulo volente*

Et non invento corpore eius, venerunt dicentes se etiam visionem angelorum vidisse... (Luke 24:23)

And having not found his body, they came, saying that they had also seen a vision of angels...

vidisse = Infinitive Perfect 'to have seen'

'Resurrection of Christ and Women at the Tomb' by Fra Angelico

READING

Symbolum Nicaenum – The Nicene Creed

Credo in unum Deum, Patrem omnipoténtem, factórem cæli et terræ, visibílium ómnium et invisibílium. Et in unum Dóminum Iesum Christum, Fílium Dei unigénitum. Et ex Patre natum ante ómnia sǽcula. Deum de Deo, lumen de lúmine, Deum verum de Deo vero. Génitum, non factum, consubstantiálem Patri: per quem ómnia facta sunt. Qui propter nos hómines et propter nostram salútem descéndit de caelis. Et incarnátus est de Spíritu Sancto ex María Vírgine: Et homo factus est. Crucifíxus étiam pro nobis: sub Póntio Piláto passus, et sepúltus est. Et resurréxit tértia die, secúndum Scriptúras. Et ascéndit in caelum: sedet ad déxteram Patris. Et íterum ventúrus est cum glória iudicáre vivos et mórtuos: cuius regni non erit finis. Et in Spíritum Sanctum, Dóminum et vivificántem: qui ex Patre Filióque procédit. Qui cum Patre et Fílio simul adorátur et conglorificátur: qui locútus est per Prophétas. Et unam sanctam cathólicam et apostólicam Ecclésiam. Confíteor unum baptísma in remissiónem peccatórum. Et exspécto resurrectiónem mortuórum. Et vitam ventúri saeculi. Amen.

factor, factōris, m (3) – maker • *baptisma, baptismatis*, n. (3) – baptism
factum – Past Participle of *faciō, facere, fēcī, factum* (3) – to make, to do
genitus – Past Participle of *genō, genere, genuī, genitum* (3) – to give birth
scrīptūra, scrīptūrae, f. (1) – book • *vīvificō, vīvificāre, vīvificāvī, vīvificātum* (1) – to revive
venturus – Future Participle – *veniō, venīre, vēnī, ventum* (4) – to come

We believe in one God, the Father, the Almighty, maker of heaven and earth, of all that is seen and unseen. We believe in one Lord, Jesus Christ, the only Son of God, eternally begotten of the Father, God from God, Light from Light, true God from true God, begotten not made, one in Being with the Father. Through him all things were made. For us men and for our salvation he came down from heaven: by the power of the Holy Spirit he was born of the Virgin Mary, and became man. For our sake he was crucified under Pontius Pilate; he suffered, died, and was buried. On the third day he rose again in fulfillment of the Scriptures; he ascended into heaven and is seated at the right hand of the Father. He will come again in glory to judge the living and the dead, and his kingdom will have no end. We believe in the Holy Spirit, the Lord, the giver of life, who proceeds from the Father and the Son. With the Father and the Son he is worshiped and glorified. He has spoken through the Prophets. We believe in one holy catholic and apostolic Church. We acknowledge one Baptism for the forgiveness of sins. We look for the resurrection of the dead and the life of the world to come. Amen.

Lesson X

Gerund and Gerundive

sapiens – making right and noble choices
prudens – practical and having good judgement,
The opposite of *prudens*: *stultus* (fool)

The **Gerund** is a Latin part of speech that is in between a noun and a verb. You can think of it as a noun formed from a verb. Let us take the Present Participle of a verb, for example,
vocare >> *vocans* – calling – replace *s* with *d* and add an ending >> *vocandum*
Vocandum is a gerund – 'calling' – the act of calling. It is singular, neuter.
credere >> *credens* >> *credendum* – things to be believed
Gerunds decline like nouns. In these familiar phrases,
modus vivendi – a way of living • *modus operandi* – a way of working
vivendi and *operandi* are the Genitive Case forms of the gerunds – *vivendum, operandum*.
Gerundive is a gerund adjective denoting what will be done, or is to be done.
It often expresses obligation or necessity.
vocandum – calling – is a gerund;
vocandus – likely / about / soon / fit to be called – is a gerundive.
Gerundives are always passive in their meaning.

ridere – to laugh
deridere – to deride, to mock
deludere – to delude, to mock

In modern European languages you find many Latin phrases and names that include gerundives:
agenda – to be done – from *agere* = to act, to do
propaganda – to be spread around – from *propagare* = to spread
memorandum – to be remembered – from *memorare* = to recall
lavender – from *lavanda* = to be washed (lavender was used to scent washed fabrics) –
from *lavare* = to wash
Amanda – fit to be loved – from *amare* = to love
Miranda – fit to be admired – from *mirari* = to admire

St. Jerome used gerunds a lot in the *Vulgata*.
Some of the most common uses are:

>>> **Purpose: ad + gerund**

MARIA, SEDENS SECUS PEDES DOMINI, AUDIEBAT VERBUM ILLIUS.

UNUM EST NECESSARIUM. MARIA OPTIMAM PARTEM ELEGIT.

DIC ILLI UT ME ADIUVET!

...*veni ad redimendum nos in brachio extento.*
...come to redeem us with an outstretched arm.
ad redimendum –
from *redimō, redimere, redēmī, redēmptum* (3) – to rescue, to redeem

Surge et accipe puerum et matrem eius, et fuge in Aegyptum et esto ibi usque dum dicam tibi futurum est enim ut Herodes quaerat puerum ad perdendum eum. (Matt. 2:13)

Arise, and take the young child and his mother, and flee into Egypt, and be there until I bring you word, for Herod will seek the young child to destroy him.

ad perdendum eum – in order to destroy him –

from *perdō, perdere, perdidī, perditum* (3) – to lose, to ruin

Et tradent eum gentibus ad deludendum et flagellandum et crucifigendum... (Matt. 20:19)

And shall deliver him to the Gentiles to mock, and to scourge, and to crucify him...

dēlūdō, dēlūdere, dēlūsī, dēlūsum (3) – to mock, to delude

flagellō, flagellāre, flagellāvī, flagellātum (1) – to fog/whip

crucīfīgō, crucīfīgere, crucīfīxī, crucīfīxum (3) – to crucify

testimonium Israel ad confitendum nomini Domini... (Psalm 121)

the testimony of Israel, to praise the name of the Lord.

ad confitendum – from *cōnfiteor, cōnfitērī, cōnfessum* (dep.) – to confess

> *ire* – to go
> *vadere* – to travel, to walk purposfully
> *ambulare* – to stroll casually

'Noli me tangere' by Fra Angelico

>>> Genitive Case gerund used in place of an infinitive that specifies the purpose/function

Qui habet aures audiendi audiat. (Matt. 13:9)
Who has ears to hear, let him hear.
audiendi – Genitive Case of the gerund *audiendum* = hearing • *aures audiendi* – ears to hear
audiat – Subjunctive Present

Gerundives are also very common in the *Vulgata*.   *credenda* – things to be believed

Dixit illis Iesus: 'Filius hominis tradendus est in manus hominum.' (Matt. 17:22)
Jesus said unto them, The Son of man shall be betrayed into the hands of men
tradendus – to be handed over – gerundive from *trādō, trādere, trādidī, trāditum* (3) – to hand over
Servum autem Domini non oportet litigare, sed mansuetum esse ad omnes, docibilem, patientem cum modestia corripientem eos qui resistunt nequando det illis Deus paenitentiam ad cognoscendam veritatem.
And the servant of the Lord must not strive; but be gentle unto all men, apt to teach, patient, in meekness instructing those that oppose themselves; if God peradventure will give them repentance to the acknowledging of the truth.
ad cognoscendam veritatem – Accusative Case feminine of
cognoscenda veritas (f.) – truth to be recognized –
cōgnōscō, cōgnōscere, cōgnōvī, cōgnitum (3) – to recognize

parvus – little (size, age...)
pusillus – insignificant
minutus – created little

Locative Case

Locative case in Latin indicates a location. It is used only with the names of cities and small islands, and does not require the preposition 'in.'
If a city name ends in - *us* or - *um*, the Locative ending is - *i*
Corinthus >> *Corinthi* = in Corinth
If a city name ends in - *a*, the Locative ending is - *ae*
Roma >> *Romae* = in Rome
If a city name ends in - *i* or - *ae*, the Locative ending is - *is*
Athenae >> *Athenis* = in Athens

Lex orandi est lex credendi et agendi.
The rule of prayer is the rule of belief and of action.

Locative case also appears with frequently-used irregular nouns, such as
domus – house >> *domi* = at home
rus – countryside >> *rure* = in the country

In *Vulgata* St. Jerome used both Locative case and in + Ablative case to indicate location.

Erat autem quidam discipulus Damasci.... (Acts 9:10)
But there was a certain disciple at Damascus . . . .
Et erat vir in Lystris infirmus pedibus. .. (Acts 14:7)
And there was a man in Lystra lame in his feet. . . .

sermo – a casual conversation
colloquium – a conversation on a particular subject
oratio – a speech, a prayer

Pluperfect and Pluperfect Subjunctive

The Latin **Pluperfect tense** describes actions that have been completed by a certain point in the past. The endings for the pluperfect are similar to present tense endings, but the stem ends in *- era*.
confirmo, confirmare, confirmavi, confirmatum (1)
confirmav + era – *confirmaveram* – I had confirmed; *confirmaveras* – you had confirmed
Pluperfect is rare in Church Latin. St. Jerome, however, often uses **Pluperfect Subjunctive** in constructions such as indirect questions and *cum* (when) + Subjunctive, e.g.:
Et cum venisset Iesus in domum principis et vidisset tibicines et turbam tumultuantem...
The Pluperfect Subjunctive is formed from the Perfect stem (the 3rd principal part of the verb):
Perfect stem + *- isse/- iss* + personal endings
video, videre, vīdī, vīsum (2) >> *vidi + isse + t* >> *vidisset*
veniō, venīre, vēnī, ventum (4) >> *veni + isse + t* >> *venisset*
portō, portāre, portāvī, portātum (1) >> *portavisset*
dīcō, dīcere, dīxī, dictum (3) >> *dixisset*

prehendere – to take an object in one's hands
capere – to capture, to lay hold of an object in order to possess it

Impersonal constructions

Oportere is an impersonal verb used a lot in the *Vulgata*.
It means ought / should / fitting / necessary.
Oportet Deo obedire magis quam hominibus. (Acts 5:29)
It is necessary to obey God, rather than men.

accipere – to accept
recipere – to adopt, to include
sumere – to take an object in order to use it

Other impersonal phrases common in the *Vulgata* include:
factum est = it came to pass • *dictum est* = it is said
Factum est autem in illis diebus, exiit in montem orare. (Luke 6:12)
And it came to pass in those days that he went out to a mountain to pray.

accidit, contigit + *ut* = it so happened that
Accidit autem ut sacerdos quidam descenderet eadem via. (Luke 10:31)
But it happened that a certain priest was going down by the same road.

necesse est = it is necessary
Necesse est enim ut veniant scandala. (Matt. 18:7)
It needs be, however, that offences come.

consecrare – to make holy, to forbid profane use
dedicare – to set apart for God

licet and *placet/conplacet* = allowed, good
Nolite timere, pusillus grex, quia conplacuit Patri vestro dare vobis regnum. (Luke 2:32)
Fear not, little flock; for it is your Father's good pleasure to give you the kingdom.

Question words *nonne* and *numquid*

In the *Vulgata* you often see two special Latin question words – *nonne* and *numquid*.
If a person who asks the question expects a positive answer, *nonne* is used – are we not / do we not.
Domine, Domine, nonne in nomine tuo prophetavimus? (Matt. 7:22)
Lord, Lord, did we not prophecy in your name?

If a person who asks the question expects a negative answer, *numquid* is used.
Respondit Pilatus: Numquid ego Judaeus sum? (John 18:35)
Pilate answered : Am I a Jew?

vita – duration of life – opposite: *mors*
salus – safety of life – opposite: *interitus* (violent death)

In the Old Testament of the *Vulgata* we also find *num* (= *numquid*).
Num custos fratris mei ego sum? (Gen. 4:9)
Am I my brother's keeper?

Notice the use of these special question words in the following passage:
Alii dicebant: Hic est Christus. Quidam autem dicebant: Numquid a Galilaea venit Christus?
Nonne scriptura dicit: Quia ex semine David ... venit Christus? (John 7:41)
Others said: This is Christ. But certain said: Does Christ come out of Galilee?
Does not the scripture say that Christ comes of the seed of David?

necesse est – natural/casual obligation • *oportet* – moral/honor obligation
opus est – a logical/rational thing to do • *debere* – moral obligation

READING

Cum autem adpropinquaret portae civitatis, et ecce, defunctus efferebatur filius unicus matri suae, et haec vidua erat, et turba civitatis multa cum illa.
Quam cum vidisset Dominus, misericordia motus super ea, dixit illi: "Noli flere!"
Et accessit, et tetigit loculum. Hii autem qui portabant steterunt, et ait: "Adulescens, tibi dico: surge!"
Et resedit qui erat mortuus, et coepit loqui, et dedit illum matri suae.
Accepit autem omnes timor. Et magnificabant Deum dicentes, quia propheta magnus surrexit in nobis et quia Deus visitavit plebem suam.
Et exiit hic sermo in universam Iudaeam de eo, et omnem circa regionem, et nuntiaverunt Iohanni discipuli eius de omnibus his. Et convocavit duos de discipulis suis Iohannes, et misit ad Dominum dicens: "Tu es qui venturus es, an alium expectamus?"
Cum autem venissent ad eum viri dixerunt: "Iohannes Baptista misit nos ad te dicens: Tu es qui venturus es, an alium expectamus?"
In ipsa autem hora curavit multos a languoribus, et plagis, et spiritibus malis, et caecis multis donavit visum.
Et respondens dixit illis: "Euntes nuntiate Iohanni quae vidistis et audistis quia caeci vident, claudi ambulant, leprosi mundantur, surdi audiunt, mortui resurgunt, pauperes evangelizantur.
(Luke 7:12-22)

Present participles:
dicens = saying (*dicere*), *respondens* = answering (*respondare*), *euntes* = going (*ire*)
Past Participles: *motus* = moved (*movere*)
Future Participle: *venturus* = who will come (*venire*)
Present Tense: *expectamus* = we expect (*expectare*), *vident* = they see (*videre*),
ambulant = they walk (*ambulare*), *mundantur* = passive: are cleaned (*mundare*),
audiunt = they hear (*audire*), *resurgunt* = arise (*resurgere*),
evangelizantur = passive: are being told good news
Past Perfect: *dixit* = he said (*dicere*), *dixerunt* = they said, *accessit* = approached (*accedere*),
tetegit = touched (*tangere*), *steterunt* = they stopped (*stare*), *resedit* = sat up/down (*residere*),
coepit = started (*coepisse*), *dedit* = gave (*dare*), *accepit* = took (*accipere*),
surrexit = arose (*surrigere*), *visitavit* = visited (*visitare*), *exiit* = came out (*exire*),
nuntiaverunt = they announced (*nuntiare*), *convocavit* = called together (*convocare*),
misit = sent (*mittere*), *curavit* = healed (*curare*), *donavit* = gave as a gift (*donare*),
vidistis = you saw (*videre*), *audistis* = you heard (*audire*)

Past Imperfect: *efferebatur* = **passive:** was carried (*efferre*), erat = was (*esse*), *portabant* = carried (*portare*), *magnificabant* = glorified (*magnificare*),
Imperative Mood:
noli flere = don't cry (*flere*), *surge* = rise (*surgere*), *nuntiate* = announce (*nuntiare*)
Subjunctive Imperfect: *adpropinquaret* = when he was approaching (*adpropinquare*)
Subjunctive Pluperfect: *vidisset* = when/after he saw (*videre*), *venissent* = when/after they came

Now when he came nigh to the gate of the city, behold, there was a dead man carried out, the only son of his mother, and she was a widow. And much people of the city was with her. And when the Lord saw her, he had compassion on her, and said unto her, "Weep not." And he came and touched the bier: and they that bare him stood still. And he said, "Young man, I say unto thee, Arise." And he that was dead sat up, and began to speak. And he delivered him to his mother. And there came a fear on all: and they glorified God, saying that a great prophet is risen up among us; and, that God has visited his people. And this rumour of him went forth throughout all Judæa, and throughout all the region round about. And the disciples of John shewed him of all these things. And John calling unto him two of his disciples sent them to Jesus, saying, "Are you he that should come? or look we for another?" When the men came to him, they said, "John Baptist has sent us to you, saying, Are you he that should come? or look we for another?" And in that same hour he cured many of their infirmities and plagues, and of evil spirits; and unto many that were blind he gave sight. Then Jesus answering said unto them, "Go your way, and tell John what things ye have seen and heard; how that the blind see, the lame walk, the lepers are cleansed, the deaf hear, the dead are raised, to the poor the gospel is preached."

The Parable of Weeds (Matt. 13:24-30)
Aliam parabolam proposuit illis dicens: Simile factum est regnum caelorum homini qui seminavit bonum semen in agro suo. Cum autem dormirent homines, venit inimicus eius et superseminavit zizania in medio tritici et abiit. Cum autem crevisset herba et fructum fecisset tunc apparuerunt et zizania. Accedentes autem servi patris familias dixerunt ei: Domine, nonne bonum semen seminasti in agro tuo unde ergo habet zizania? Et ait illis: Inimicus homo hoc fecit. Servi autem dixerunt ei: Vis, imus, et colligimus ea? Et ait: Non. Ne forte colligentes zizania, eradicetis simul cum eis et triticum. Sinite utraque crescere usque ad messem et in tempore messis dicam messoribus: Colligite primum zizania, et alligate ea in fasciculos ad conburendum. Triticum autem congregate in horreum meum.

ager, agrī, m. (2) – field • *inimīcus, inimīcī,* m. (2) – enemy • *trīticum, trīticī,* n. (2) – wheat
zīzania, zīzaniōrum, n. (2) – weed • *servus, servī,* m. (2) – slave, servant
messis, messis, m. (3) – harvest
proposuit – Past Perfect – *prōpōnō, prōpōnere, prōposuī, prōpositum* (3) – to put forward
seminavit – Pasts Perfect – *sēminō, sēmināre, sēmināvī, sēminātum* (1) – to plant
dormirent – Subjunctive – *dormiō, dormīre, dormīvī, dormītum* (4) – to sleep
venit – Past Perfect – *veniō, venīre, vēnī, ventum* (4) – to come
abiit – Past Perfect – *abeō, abīre, abiī / abivī, abitum* (irr.) – to leave
crevisset – Subjunctive Pluperfect – *crēscō, crēscere, crēvī, crētum* (3) – to grow
fecisset – Subjunctive Pluperfect – *faciō, facere, fēcī, factum* (3) – to make, to do
apparuerunt – Past Perfect – *appāreō, appārēre, appāruī, appāritum* (2) – to appear
accedentes – Present Participle, plural – *accēdō, accēdere, accessī, accessum* (3) – to approach
dixerunt – Past Perfect – *dīcō, dīcere, dīxī, dictum* (3) – to say
ait – Past Perfect – *āiō, āiere* (3) – to confirm, to say 'yes'
fecit – Past Perfect – *facere*
vis – Present Tense – *volō, velle, voluī* (irr.) – to want
colligimus – Present tense – *colligō, colligere, collēgī, collēctum* (3) – to collect
colligentes – Present participle, plural
eradicetis – Subjunctive Present – *colligō, colligere, collēgī, collēctum* (3) – to root out
sinite – Imperative Mood, plural – *sinō, sinere, sīvī, situm* (3) – allow
dicam – Simple Future – *dicere*
alligate – Imperative Mood – *alligō, alligāre, alligāvī, alligātum* (1) – to bind
ad comburendum – gerund – *combūrō, combūrere, combussī, combustum* (3) – to burn up

Jesus told them another parable: "The kingdom of heaven is like a man who sowed good seed in his field. But while everyone was sleeping, his enemy came and sowed weeds among the wheat, and went away. When the wheat sprouted and formed heads, then the weeds also appeared. 'The owner's servants came to him and said, 'Sir, didn't you sow good seed in your field? Where then did the weeds come from?' 'An enemy did this,' he replied. The servants asked him, 'Do you want us to go and pull them up?' 'No,' he answered, 'because while you are pulling the weeds, you may uproot the wheat with them. Let both grow together until the harvest. At that time I will tell the harvesters: First collect the weeds and tie them in bundles to be burned; then gather the wheat and bring it into my barn.'"

GRAMMAR INDEX

LESSON I Nouns and adjectives: number, gender, declension
LESSON II Personal and possessive pronouns; Genitive case, Ablative case; prepositions
LESSON III Vocative case; Verbs: Conjugation, Present tense, Imperative Mood, *esse*
LESSON IV Past tense: Perfect and Imperfect; conjunctions
LESSON V Accusative Case, Dative Case
LESSON VI Relative pronouns, Participles
LESSON VII *Posse, Ire, velle/nolle*; Subjunctive Mood
LESSON VIII Future Tense; Passive voice; deponent verbs
LESSON IX Comparative degrees of adjectives and adverbs; special uses of the Ablative case (comparison, instrumental, absolute)
LESSON X Gerund, gerundive

CHARTS

Noun declension – all cases, all declensions – Lesson V
Pronouns declension – all cases – Lesson VI
Present participles declension – Lesson VI
Past and Future participles declension – Lesson VI

Present tense verb endings – Lesson III
Imperfect and Perfect Past tense verb endings – Lesson IV
Future tense verb endings – Lesson VIII
Subjunctive Mood verb endings – Lesson VII
Passive Voice verb endings – Lesson VIII

esse, posse, ire, velle/nolle – Present, Past Perfect and Imperfect endings – Lesson VII
esse – Simple Future tense endings – Lesson VIII
esse, posse – Future Perfect tense endings – Lesson VIII
esse – Subjunctive Present, Imperfect, Perfect – Lesson VII

Latin conjunctions – Lesson IV

Books for Further Study

Most of the books in this list are available for download in various formats at the *Internet Archive*.

A Grammar of the Vulgate by W. E. Plater and H. J. White, Clarendon Press, 1926
Ecclesiastical Dictionary by John Thein, Benziger Brothers, 1900
A Dictionary of the Psalter by Dom Matthew Britt, Benziger Brothers, 1928
Döderlein's Handbook of Latin Synonyms, W.F.Draper, 1875
An Introduction to Ecclesiastical Latin by Rev. H.P.V. Nunn, Cambridge University Press, 1922
A Primer of Medieval Latin by Charles H. Benson, Scott, Foresman & Co. 1925
School Grammar of the Latin Language by C.G. Zumpt, Longman 1846
Grammar of the Latin Language by Leonhard Schmitz, W. and R. Chambers, 1863
A First Latin Book for Catholic Schools by Roy Joseph Deferrari, The Catholic Education Press, 1921
Latin Language and Grammar for Children by Angus Dallas, Hunter, Rose & Co., 1978
A Manual of Prayers for the Use of the Catholic Laity, Christian Press Association, 1896
Selections from Early Christian Writers by Henry Melvill Gwatkin, Macmillan, 1902
The Liber Usualis, by the Benedictines of Solesmes, Desclee Company, 1961
Latin Hymns with English Notes by F.A. March, Harper and Brothers, 1894
Latin Hymns by Matthew Germing, Loyola University Press, 1920
St. Basil's Hymnal compiled by the Basilian Brothers, John P. Daleiden, 1918
Catholic Hymnal by Rev. John G. Hacker, Schwartz, Kirwin & Fauss, 1920
Catholic Hours, the Family Prayer Book, T. Jones, Catholic Publisher, 1840
Poems, Charades, Inscriptions by Pope Leo XIII, by H.T. Henry, The Dolphin Press, 1902
Know Your Mass by Fr. Demetrius Manousos & Addison Burbank, 1954
The Mass in Slow Motion by Ronald Knox, Sheed & Ward, 1948